SOCIAL MEDIA MASTERY

TWO MANUSCRIPTS

FACEBOOK ADVERTISING & INSTAGRAM MARKETING. BEST PRACTICES FOR INFLUENCERS, YOUR BRAND, AND YOUR BUSINESS.

FACEBOOK ADVERTISING

WHY AREN'T YOU MAKING SALES with FB ADVERTISING? MARKETING TO TURN ADS INTO PROFITS

medical or professional advice. The content within this book has been derived from various sources. Please consult a licensed professional before attempting any techniques outlined in this book.

By reading this document, the reader agrees that under no circumstances is the author responsible for any losses, direct or indirect, which are incurred as a result of the use of information contained within this document, including, but not limited to, — errors, omissions, or inaccuracies.

TABLE OF CONTENTS

INTRODUCTION

I want to thank you for choosing this book "Facebook Advertising: Why Aren't You Making Sales with FB Advertising? Marketing to Turn Ads into Profits."

Facebook is one of the largest social media platforms at present. In fact, it boasts of over 2 billion active users every month. Taking into consideration these figures, it is not hard to imagine why a lot of businesses - both big and small, have chosen Facebook as a means to interact and engage with their users. If you are still not on the Facebook bandwagon, then it is time for you to jump onto it right away!

The way brands and customers have been interacting in the 21st century has changed. Customers expect brands to use different marketing techniques for making their products or services seem more appealing. There has been a steep increase in the use of visual communication for marketing and advertising that has caused different businesses to use different promotional strategies. This is where social media marketing steps in. Almost everyone these days makes use of social media, and brands are making use of these platforms for marketing themselves. One of the most popular social media platforms is Facebook. It has over a billion active users and has immense potential. An upcoming and quite successful practice that brands are making use of is Facebook marketing.

Numerous brands have started using Facebook as a "me too" strategy to cover all their bases on social media as well. Not many have however, taken the time, or put in the effort for understanding the best way in which this platform can be made use of. It is important to understand this platform if you want to make the most of its marketing potential. Consumers are always active on Facebook, and it is up to the brands to choose the way they can target their potential clientele. Marketers must learn to become a visual teller of tales and artists on Facebook to communicate effectively with consumers. It is important to combine elements of storytelling art and strategies to develop content, which will help brands, connect with consumers on Facebook through a clear message. This will help to produce extremely good results.

If you want to learn all about the ways in which Facebook will benefit your business, and want to start using Facebook advertising, then you have come to the right place. If you want to learn to make the most of all that Facebook has to offer, then this is the perfect book for you. In this book, you will learn everything that you need to know about Facebook advertising. You will learn about the ways in which Facebook helps businesses, the fundamentals of Facebook advertising, tips to build a community, about Facebook marketing, tips for Facebook advertising, tips for developing high-quality content, Facebook resources, and much more. If you are ready to learn about all of this, then let us start without further ado.

Chapter One: How Facebook is Shaping Businesses

Quickly Reach the Target Audience

With Facebook, you will be able to reach a lot of people within no time. It isn't just about making your product information available to all these people; it is about being able to reach your target audience as quickly as possible. Facebook will help you reach your target audience within no time. Facebook also provides you with the option of customizing your audience.

Targeted Business Activity

You have the option of targeting your business activities on Facebook depending upon the popular trends, and also an analysis of the strategy used by your competitors at different times.

Transparency in a Business Relationship

By creating business pages on Facebook, you can build open relationships with your customers. Such transparency reflects well on your business ethics, and it will also help in the acquisition and retainment of a customer base that is loyal.

EASE

Facebook makes it easy to search for your business, brand, products and services that you offer. Almost everyone seems to have a Facebook account these days, regardless of their age. People tend to spend a while browsing through different product pages on this site. If you have a Facebook page, it will certainly be easier for your audience to find you. It is definitely easier than searching for the address of your business website or on the web.

CHAT ROOMS

Facebook provides the option of chatting with your customers or clients on your business page on Facebook. Their grievances, complaints, and concerns can be addressed immediately. It helps to maintain clarity about the business practices and helps in establishing trust and inspiring loyalty amongst the customers.

Zero-Cost Sharing

You can share information about your products and services in real time, without having to worry about the costs that you will have to incur. Free advertisement is the best sort of advertisement there is.

Viral Promotion

Facebook users can share your business page and even post it on their Facebook accounts. If you can influence your brand message or the activities, then they will, in turn, influence all their followers to see your page as well. It can have a cascading effect, and increase the traffic to your page. This is exactly what viral marketing is all about, and you can capitalize on it with the help of Facebook.

Target Interested Persons

You have the option of targeting those people who are interested in what you are offering. Since these people have willingly become a part of your Facebook page, it will help if you can offer them special notifications about any upcoming offers or promotional offers and the like, before others get it. For instance, an invitation to a product launch event can be sent to hundreds of people, but, if you offer a special discount to all those who register early, then this will certainly attract more crowds.

Just because there are over a billion active users, it doesn't mean that they will all want to 'like' your page. It doesn't make sense to engage everyone on Facebook. It only makes sense to engage your target audience and Facebook helps you do this. Once you are aware of this, creating a marketing strategy by keeping them in mind isn't all that difficult. You can get 'likes' easily by targeting your ads. You will need to target those users who are interested in what you offer, or something similar. If you have a local business, then you must target your ads so that they will reach potential customers who live within a radius of 10-15 miles. The ads might be slightly costly, but the likelihood of reaching out to your potential customers is higher. Running an ad on TV, or even a local newspaper, is not only expensive, but you will never be sure of whether it has reached the intended audience or not. With Facebook ads, you can be certain of this, provided you target your ad properly.

Social Media Proof

Social media proof is quite important for any business. The number of 'likes,' 'shares,' and 'comments' you get will help in the growth of your online presence. It will also provide you with the confidence necessary to work on a wider range of products or services. All these 'likes' and 'shares' can also help you in judging whether or not the public approves of them.

UNDERSTANDING CUSTOMER BEHAVIOR

You can understand the kind of things that grab the attention of your audience and the kind of things that trigger their liking. It will help a business develop a marketing and a promotional strategy that takes into consideration the needs and likes of its customers. You can use Google analytics to do the same.

DATA INSIGHTS

Facebook helps provide data insights about functionality so that you can track and analyze whether your marketing and advertising efforts are paying off or not. These are quite helpful when it comes to decision-making. In fact, they were developed with the intention of helping businesses so that they can get a detailed analysis of the traffic that visits their page. Data insights can make considerable changes to the marketing strategy of any business.

GATHERING MORE LEADS

It isn't enough if people merely like your page if you want to provide yourself with a long-term business that is sustainable. Yes, it is true that you can earn yourself a good short-term living with the help of your Facebook page, but, what can you do in case something goes wrong with your Facebook page? You need to be able to strike a connection with your customers that goes beyond Facebook. Smart businesses will gather leads by collecting email addresses so that they can contact their customers outside Facebook as well. All this is usually done via contests, giveaways, and newsletters as well; however, you need to be careful about the way you use all these leads. For instance, you must not spam your fans or clients with junk mail. Email them maybe once or twice a week and make sure that the information you are providing is helpful to them, and will convince them to become customers, instead of pushing them away.

REDUCTION IN YOUR MARKETING EXPENSES

You needn't spend anything to start your own Facebook business page. If you feel like it, then you can hire a graphic designer to design your profile picture and the cover photo; however, this isn't necessary. You can simply take pictures of your business and that will be fine. Until you start paying for ads for getting 'likes' for your page, you needn't spend anything to set your page up. When compared to conventional ads, Facebook ads are quite inexpensive and will help you reach a wider audience. As the number of people who are engaging on your page increase, so will the visibility of your page. It will help you garner more attention without having to do much. If you target your ads towards all those who are interested in your page, then you can reduce your costs.

USE FACEBOOK INSIGHTS

Some people are naturally good with numbers, and then there are those who need some help figuring out all the data that they are provided with; Facebook Insights helps in simplifying this. Not only is the information provided easy to understand, but it also provides helpful information for business owners. Anyone can understand the data that has been provided here. Insights will provide you with information about the number of 'likes' the page has received, the reach of all the posts and the page, engagement of the page and much more. You can check how a particular post is performing, the general demographics of your fans and so on. It is easy to analyze the results provided by Insights, and you don't have to be a technical wiz to figure things out. Compare this to the traditional ads, and Facebook Insights is much more helpful. All this data comes in handy when you develop your marketing and advertising strategies.

ESTABLISHES BRAND LOYALTY

Apart from building a customer base and selling products, your Facebook page can help you build brand loyalty. What exactly does brand loyalty mean? Well, if you provide valuable and engaging content consistently, then your followers will stay loyal and will overlook the mistakes you make. These days, people are keen on finding businesses from which they can buy, and for searching, they often turn to social media. If your followers can see that your brand or business is quite active and responsive online, then the likelihood of them doing business with you is higher than that of a company that doesn't have any Facebook presence or has a page that is poorly managed. In this age of technology that we live in, the Internet has become a major part of our lives. Social media has become a convenient substitute for real-time conversations. People tend to turn towards social media about opinions regarding various things. If your brand has a social media presence, then your chances of attracting new customers and retaining the existing ones are higher.

INCREASES YOUR WEB TRAFFIC

A smart Facebook page owner will make use of their Facebook page for directing traffic towards their websites. If you want to be a good marketer, then you need to do more than just engaging viewers on the page so, you need to start posting links, along with the posts, for driving the traffic towards your website. One great thing about link posts is that Facebook now produces a full-width thumbnail if your website has one. Since they attract more attention, it is likely that these images have a higher probability of getting clicked. A good content strategy must include posting of links to your website. You can post twice a day about content related to your website, and mix this in with a couple of other light-hearted posts that will help in engaging the audience. If you have a proper posting strategy while posting content on Facebook, then you can increase your web traffic. You will need to constantly come up with different ways in which you can do this.

PROMOTING SEARCH ENGINE OPTIMIZATION (SEO)

SEO, and its relation to Facebook, is a topic that is frequently debated upon. Some believe that the information that one will include in the "About" section of the business page can be scraped and, therefore, it can be searched on Google. Well, it is difficult to verify or deny this claim. If you run a simple Google search for your business page, then the Facebook page of your business will be one of the first results displayed, if you do have a Facebook page. In marketing, it does help if more people can easily find you. All this is good for your business, and a Facebook page will help improve your online visibility.

BEING MOBILE READY

Most of the Facebook users are accessing this social media platform via their mobile devices; this will include their smartphones and tablets. As this trend starts to grow, it becomes increasingly important for your business to be present on Facebook. A good thing about a Facebook page is that Facebook will do all the heavy lifting for you. It means that your Facebook page will automatically be optimized for viewing on a desktop or a mobile device, depending upon the device that the user uses for accessing it. The exception to this one will be the tab that will display custom apps on your business page that can be seen when accessing Facebook via your desktop, but not on the mobile devices (unless you provide links that are mobile friendly). When users view your Facebook business page on their mobile device, then it will show them the hours of operation, address, any reviews, and phone numbers and so on. You will need to make sure that you are including useful information on your page.

KEEPING AN EYE ON YOUR COMPETITION

Facebook has a new feature that will allow you to keep an eye on your competition within the market. It is a really good way for seeing how your competitors and others in your niche are growing on this social media platform. You have the option of customizing your feed. You can add a list of your competitors to this, and keep an eye on their performance. Facebook will also provide you with a list of suggestions regarding similar businesses in your area, and you can include these by clicking on the "Watch Page" option. You can select 5 or more than 5 pages depending on your preference. If you look at pages in this option, then you will get to know if there is an explosion of activity or engagement with users on the page, then, in such a case, you can check to see what is it that they are doing. This will help you in coming up with new ideas that might work for you as well.

CHAPTER TWO:
FUNDAMENTALS

There are three fundamental aspects of Facebook, and you will learn all about them in this section.

1#BUILD AN AUDIENCE

If you want to build an audience for your Facebook page from scratch, then use the tips mentioned in this section.

ESTABLISH A ROUTINE

You need to make sure that the content publishing routine that you opt for appeals to your target audience so, do you know about your target audience? If you don't, then here are a couple of questions that will help you understand your target audience. How old is your ideal customer base? What is their gender? Where do they live? What is the kind of content that they value? What are the usual questions they ask? You need to establish a routine to publish your content. If you have a structure, then you can make sure that the content reaches the target audience. Your goal is to not just reach your current users, but to engage them so that the word about your business spreads.

GRAPH SEARCH

Graph Search is a brilliant tool that you can use to learn about your brand's audience. If you don't have an established audience, then you need to learn more about the users who frequent the pages related to the products or services that you offer, or similar pages. The first thing that you need to do is come up with two Facebook pages that are either your competitors or quite similar to yours. Then you need to run a search about the pages that their fans like. For instance, search for "Pages liked by people who like Nike and Reebok." The search results for this entry will help you analyze the kind of content that interests your target audience.

HIGHLY-TARGETED FACEBOOK ADS

All the information that you gathered in the previous step will come in handy now. Whenever you decide to run any Facebook ads, then you need to make sure that they are highly targeted so, ensure that they only surface on the pages of all those people who fit your ideal demographic. You can control it with the help of basic features like their age, location, career, preferences, and gender and so on.

PREMIUM CONTENT

You need to create something of value that will appeal to your target audience. You cannot expect to build an audience if you don't offer them something appealing. You need to offer them some free premium content so that they stay loyal to your brand.

HASHTAGS

Using hashtags on Facebook has gained a lot of traction. It is a great way to reach a broader audience. You can research the hashtags that are currently trending in your niche, and you can use the same to broaden your reach. Use hashtags that are appropriate for the content you offer. Whenever a Facebook user searches for a hashtag, all the pages that are related to that particular hashtag show up in the search results. It is a simple and effective manner to improve your online visibility.

NETWORK

If you haven't been networking until now, you need to start doing it immediately. You need to be able to look beyond Facebook if you really want to promote your business and create a large audience base. Work on collaborating with bloggers, vloggers and influencers on other social media sites to direct leads to your Facebook page.

2# ENGAGEMENT

Once you build an audience base for yourself, your job doesn't end. You need to retain your current audience and gain a larger audience base. To do this, you need to learn to boost Facebook engagement. In this section, you will learn about certain simple things that you can do to boost your Facebook engagement.

YOUR PERSONALITY

Social media is about being social. No one will want to interact with a media bot; instead, you need to work on showcasing your business or your brand's personality through your Facebook posts. You need to make your business seem sociable to your audience, only then will they want to engage with it.

ASK QUESTIONS

If you want people to engage with your posts, then a simple manner of doing this is by asking questions. You can ask your fans and followers certain questions and wait for their answers. You can ask them questions about anything, but make sure that the questions you ask aren't too technical and keep

28

them casual. The idea is to get your followers to start talking.

IMAGES

A picture is worth a thousand words. You can convey a powerful message through a couple of stories. Not just that, stories look attractive when compared to text so, take some photos to promote your business or your brand, and then post them on Facebook. It will also help your followers understand what your business is all about.

SNEAK PEEK

An amazing thing about using Facebook as a marketing tool is that you can promote your business without seeming too promotional. You can post snapshots of employees, of customers, of your daily operations and much more. In a way, these images help lend a human-like feel to your business.

SPECIFIC

You need to pay attention to the kind of content that your audience responds to. Not just that, you also need to concentrate on the posting time to maximize the number of likes, shares and comments your posts garner. The greater number of 'likes,' 'shares,' and 'comments' you receive on your posts, the wider your potential base of audience will be.

FAN'S CONTENT

Social media is all about sharing. The easiest way to build a relationship on social media is by sharing so, if you ever come across any useful content, even if it is from other businesses, don't be hesitant to share. Share the news with your followers. Everyone values good and useful content, but don't overshare.

SIMPLE POSTS

At times, a simple text-only status can have a huge impact. You don't always have to share a ton of information or lengthy posts. A simple post will do the trick. Regardless of what you decide to do, have some fun. Don't make it all about business. If you want your follower base to grow, then you need to make the page fun.

3# CONVERSION

Facebook boasts of over 650 million daily visitors. Well, the statistics are quite favorable if you are working on conversions. Conversion occurs when someone interacts with an ad you post and then takes action on it in a manner that is favorable for your business. It might refer to an online purchase, or even a call to your business.

One of the most critical metrics for a social marketer to track on Facebook is the conversion rate. Conversion rate refers to the point at which a user decides to convert from an ordinary browser to a buyer. For most marketers, conversion is a top priority. In fact, a good conversion rate is a measure of success. Conversion isn't always about driving purchases; it is also about driving action. The goal of a campaign can be to increase the subscription for weekly newsletters or to encourage shoppers to add more products to their wishlist. Facebook is one of the best platforms to drive conversions. In this section, you will learn about the different ways in which you can increase your rate of conversion.

DEFINE THE CONVERSION EVENT

Before you think about conversions, the first thing that you need to decide is the action that people need to take after they see the ad. Different types of conversion that Facebook supports include viewing content, adding products to the wishlist, initiating checkout and purchases. You can even create custom-made conversion events if you have a specific goal in mind. You cannot expect a single ad to meet all your conversion goals. You need to create different ads to meet different goals.

Don't Forget About the Destination

There is a direct relationship between the ad and the landing page. The ad is only as good as the landing page is. When you decide the place of conversion, you need to ensure that everything is in place to deliver on all that the ad promises. Here are a couple of things that you must keep in mind when you prepare the landing page. You need to implement Pixel if you want to track the event. Once you identify the landing page, then you need to add the Facebook Pixel code to it to track the event. There needs to be continuity between the ad and the landing page. For instance, if the ad is about shoes and the landing page takes the customer to a page about trousers, it defeats the purpose of the ad. A lot of people these days tend to make online purchases on their smartphones, so it makes sense to direct the traffic to your app, so you need to work on app optimization to increase your conversion rate.

Visuals

It takes a user about 2.6 seconds to decide where to land on a webpage, so you need to use eye-catching visuals to attract your potential customers. The first impression that a user has about your business or your brand is by the design they see. The visuals in an ad are quite similar to a handshake. There are a couple of things that you need to keep in mind when you design the visuals for an ad. You need to make sure that you don't overload images along with the text. It is a good idea to sparingly use text in images. If you overcrowd the ad with images and texts, it will look chaotic and the chances are that the potential customer will scroll past it. The visuals need to be of high-resolution, and any low-resolution visuals will convey a poor image of your brand. Imagery with movement is better than static imagery, so you can opt for GIFs whenever possible.

Short and Sweet

If there is too much content in an ad, the rate of conversion will be quite low so you need to keep the copy short and simple. Try to use personal pronouns (like we) to create a relationship between the audience and the business. Try to avoid any technical jargon and keep it brief. Brief text looks inviting, and too much text can seem quite overwhelming.

Call-to-Action

Conversion is all about motivating an action; therefore, you need to include a call-to-action in the ad. You can use effective verbs like start, find, explore or even discover to improve your conversion rate. If your aim is to increase purchases or subscriptions, then you can use phrases like "buy now," "register now" or "sign up now."

AUDIENCE

When you create an ad, you need to opt for targeting expansion. When you opt for this, then Facebook will help you find more users with similar interests. Not just that, it also allows you to broaden your base of audience and reach out to more people. The larger your audience is, the higher your rate of conversion will be.

OPTIMIZE FOR CONVERSIONS

By now, you are aware of different things that you can do to optimize your conversions, but the one thing that you must do without fail is to tick the "conversions" box on Facebook. Go to the Budget and Schedule form→ "optimization for delivery" section→ check off "conversions."

THE FORMAT OF THE AD

According to the goals of your ad campaign, you need to select a particular format of a Facebook ad. There are some that might serve a particular ad campaign better than the other options. For instance, Adidas used the video with Facebook's collection feature, which helped them to showcase various features of the Z.N.E Road Trip Hoodie and decreased their overall cost-per-conversion. Here are a couple of things that you need to consider when you decide the ad format. You can use a Carousel or collection ads when you need to showcase multiple products, or need to display various features. The Facebook Offer ads are a good idea if you want to broadcast about any special deals or any discounts to use as an incentive for purchase. If you want to use high-impact visuals and experiences that look good on a full-screen, then opt for Facebook Canvas.

Chapter Three: The Importance of Building a Community

Facebook isn't about individuals, it's about community. Facebook is a means to communicate and get in touch with others. It is a global social platform to meet like-minded people. A Facebook community helps build awareness about your business or your brand, and it creates excitement about your products or services and promotes your business; therefore, it is important that you build a community for your business on Facebook. In this section, you will learn more about it.

It is Not about You

Most businesses usually have the pressure to maximize their sales through marketing. You need to remember that Facebook communities are not the place for you to pitch. Groups on Facebook are not about you. Your community is not your target audience. If the conversation is essentially between you and the members of your community, then your community is your audience. If the conversation is primarily between the members of the group, then such a group is your community and not your audience. A Facebook community consists of people who form relationships that arise from their shared goals, experiences or their interests. Your community is merely a portion of your market, and those members need to be targeted for their interest in all that you offer and where they exist in the customer journey. It does mean that they need to have some experience with your business or brand, the services you offer, and their needs must match your USP. The primary focus in a community is the relationship they share with each other and not your business. Your role is that of a facilitator and your aim is to let the conversations grow. You can do this by asking questions and encouraging conversations. You need to get better acquainted with all those in your community. You can do this by welcoming people, introducing people with common needs, being patient and waiting for that connection to continue to build.

MAINTAIN EXCLUSIVITY

Who doesn't like the feel of exclusivity? Everybody likes it when they feel like they have exclusive access to something. Well, that's the wonderful thing about Facebook groups. Exclusivity helps create a stronger relationship with not just the fellow members, but with your business as well. For instance, doesn't it make you feel pretty fancy when you have a membership card to an exclusive club? Well, the same logic applies to Facebook communities as well. The more exclusive the group is, the more the members will have in common and their engagement increases naturally. You can control the access by putting in certain rules for registration and vet the members before you accept them. The result of all this? The members will feel like they are part of something exclusive. You might wonder why it matters. For starters, this encourages the members to discuss and promote your business and you don't even have to pitch to them. They automatically assume the role of brand advocates.

AVOID BEING A SALESPERSON

When it is the time to make a purchase, people tend to become picky. What do they want to see? Most of the customers prefer peer recommendations above any professionally written content. Content that is created by peers is certainly more effective than the one that the brand creates. By nature, people tend to trust their peers more than they trust the brand. The members of a community will automatically support your brand or business when they feel that they are being supported and their support is valued. You need to deliver on the promises you make, and the support will flow in steadily.

Don't Air Your Dirty Laundry

Your role as a community manager is to moderate and encourage discussion. The members need to feel that the community is a place where they can share their views and insights without any judgment. Whenever a disagreement crops up in the community, then, as a community manager, you need to have a plan to disperse the heated discussion quickly. You need to monitor the group activities carefully and you need to have someone in place who will respond promptly and empathetically to any disagreements.

New Members

If there are no new additions to the community, then the turnover and the conversion that the Facebook group attracts will become stagnant. You need to infuse new members into the community. When you accept new members, you need to show them some love. You need to make the new members feel welcome, and you need to readily involve them in discussions. You can do this by selecting a couple of standardized questions that you can ask them as soon as they are part of the group. You can find a buddy for the new members and make them feel comfortable.

LOYALTY

There are four things that the members of a strong community need to feel, and these are:

- They need to feel exclusive.
- They need to benefit from the influence.
- They need to feel an emotional connection.
- Their needs need to be fulfilled.

Members need to be able to recognize each other and, for this, you can create logos or the like. Facebook helps with this by referencing group membership. Members need to feel that their actions can influence the group and that the group can influence their actions. To manage all this, it is a good idea to have a group policy and understand the group jargon. Recognition and rewards are the best means to reward any participation. If you build a loyal community for your brand, it automatically leads to a better rate of conversion.

CELEBRATE

If you want to increase positive activity in the group, then you need to include some public praise. When you do praise someone, make sure that you convey your gratitude to them. You can send them a card, chocolates or any other small token of appreciation that says, "Thank you for being a valuable member of the community."

COMMUNITY

Business owners usually care only about their revenues and costs; however, there are four elements of social media and these elements are valid for community management as well. Your community helps with indirect selling and you need to optimize it. The four elements that you need to concentrate on are social listening, social influencing, social networking and social selling.

Social listening is all about monitoring, responding and providing customer service on a social platform. Social listening helps to fill in any gaps between content, products, marketing and resolving issues that were not known to the brand or the community manager. Social influencing is the act of establishing an authority on social media platforms through the distribution of content that is helpful and practical. Social networking refers to finding influencers to advocate your brand. Social selling is the act of indirectly finding leads that will result in conversions. The best way to increase your sales is by building constructive feedback.

If you want to increase sales, increase brand visibility, develop a strong audience base and improve the rate of conversion, then you need to have a strong community.

Chapter Four: Facebook Marketing

The growth of Facebook isn't going to slow down. If anything, it is steadily increasing in popularity and Facebook marketing has become the new marketing tactic so, if you want to start marketing on Facebook, you will need to have a strategy in mind. In this chapter, let us take a look at the manner in which you can develop a marketing strategy for your business on Facebook.

Your Goals

No strategy can be penned down without having certain goals in mind. The same applies to Facebook marketing as well. Goals will help you in establishing the actual marketing needs of your business. If you want to make use of Facebook for marketing, or for improving an existing strategy, then you have some needs in mind. Don't set unrealistic goals that depend on vanity metrics like the number of 'likes' or the number of followers; instead, you must address your main challenges. For a business, some goals will be increasing the quality of sales, value addition to the organization, getting a better pulse of the industry, and better growth. Facebook can indeed help in achieving these goals. The first step in improving the quality of sales will be through better targeting. If you have a well thought out Facebook marketing strategy, then you can reach your target audience quite effectively. Don't work under the assumption that the bigger the pond is the bigger fish you will get to catch. You need to understand that Facebook is just a means by which you can achieve your goals. Facebook can be made use of for nurturing the relationship of the business with its customers, for creating and improving awareness, and also for providing better resources to your audience.

Does it feel like your competitors are always a step ahead of you? Well, you can start making various social media monitoring tools that can help you in tracking the movement of your competitors on the market. Social recruiting isn't easy, but it certainly is becoming quite a popular technique these days. Social media, especially Facebook, can be made use of for making recruiting an easier process. Smarter growth will imply an increase in acquisition, reduction in churn, and a decrease in spending. Well, Facebook can help in achieving all this. Facebook helps in the reduction of ad spending, increased targeting and better social selling. These things, when incorporated into your Facebook marketing strategy, can help you in achieving the organizational goals that you might have set for yourself. Facebook marketing will help you in achieving these objectives with lesser effort than the conventional methods will take. It is all about working smarter these days, not harder.

STUDYING THE FACEBOOK DEMOGRAPHICS

Demographics are an important element of any marketing strategy and Facebook marketing is no different. When you take the vast reach of Facebook, you realize that there are over 1.6 billion registered users who are going through their newsfeed daily, so it is quite important to figure out the manner in which you can reach them. Also, it is quite important to understand the latest demographics of the users since these figures keep fluctuating. Age and gender is no bar when it comes to using Facebook. Anyone with an Internet connection and a smartphone can create a profile for themselves on this network. Facebook is no longer restricted to only the younger generation. Don't be under the misconception that only the 18 to 25 year-olds are active on Facebook. Facebook's demographics are spread all across the world. There is so much versatility that it presents a business with, so try to make the most of it. Your business has access to an international portal that transcends all physical boundaries. This is the best platform for implementing a marketing strategy to target your audience regardless of their location.

SELECTING AND SCHEDULING YOUR FACEBOOK CONTENT

Every social networking platform has its own style of content; however, Facebook is quite versatile. Your brand has plenty of content strategies to choose from. There is the option of Facebook Stories, Live, images, videos, or even just regular content. The opportunities it has to offer are unlimited. For a business, all that matters will be the quality of the content that is being published, along with the audience and their expectations from the Facebook page of your business. Remember that you need to be active while promoting your business but must not go overboard. Your Facebook page must not be like the used-car-lot with a lot of aggressive salesmen. The content that you choose to post must be informative, entertaining, and compelling. It must be of some value to the audience. Your Facebook page needs to encourage promotions, but it must not be just restricted to that. You need to highlight the values of your brand, identify your target audience, and also create a space that is quite unique and specific to your business or brand.

Now that you know the importance of content, you need to figure out a form of content that will work well for you. Let us take a look at the different types of content to choose from, and the best way in which you can use them.

Status: This is perhaps the simplest form of communication that is available on this platform. If used properly, it can be quite effective as well. With the addition of several new features that enable you to change the text size and select a background color, you can make the status stand out and quite attractive.

Images: Posts that have images in them are more effective when it comes to the rate of engagement generated. Don't just rely on images to do all the work for you. You will need to use images that are of a high quality and will wow your audience. It needs to be tasteful, creative, and attractive. It is the only way in which you can grab the attention of your audience.

Videos: Videos are in good demand these days, but only a few users actually watch the video with sound, like it is supposed to be viewed. The video posted must not be too long, it must be easy to understand, and always have captions in it. The video must never make the user feel like it was a waste of their time.

Links: These are the perfect means of sharing news related to the industry and your business. You need to find content that is quite engaging, and share the links to only such content.

Facebook Live: This method gets the most engagement on Facebook. With the growth of 'in the moment' content, your brand or business can give sneak peeks into your world in real time! If there is a product launch, you can just go live with it! This will help in attracting the attention of a larger audience.

Facebook Stories: If you are a Snapchat user, then you must be aware of Snapchat stories. In the same manner, Facebook has come up with Facebook Stories. Your story on Facebook can consist of small clips that can be viewed by a user at any point in time.

Once you have figured out the content that you will want to use, you will need to schedule a time for posting this content. The last thing that you will want to do is publish haphazard content, just for the sake of posting something. Planning content means that you will think through before publishing the content and this will help in making sure that the content being posted is of good quality. It also improves the chances of your business engaging the audience but, at times, you might not have any time for creating content. In such a case, you can make use of social media publishing tools like Sprout Social for helping you develop content for your Facebook page. Don't rush to schedule a post, take time, go through the content and then decide about when it must be posted.

FACEBOOK ADS STRATEGY

Your Facebook Ads strategy must be such that it will help in increasing the awareness of your brand. There are two things that you must consider when you design the Facebook ad campaign, and these are cost-effectiveness and relevancy. Well, you will need to stay well within your allocated budget for marketing. A budget is important if you want to avoid any unnecessary clicks or overexposure. If you aren't spending wisely, then it might just defeat the whole purpose of marketing on social media. The Facebook ad that you are making use of needs to be relevant as well. Targeting a wide audience isn't necessarily a bad thing; however, what might be relevant to one group might not be relevant to the other one. If you are aware of your target audience, then you can design ads keeping in mind their requirements. This will make more sense than just developing content for a random audience.

Start interacting and don't wait for your audience to take the first step

You need to remember that Facebook is a social networking platform. The basis of any such platform is communication and interaction, so interact with your audience and don't just wait for them to take the first step. If you are passive in this aspect, then it will discourage your audience as well. Well, you certainly don't need this. Start interacting with your existing and potential customers. Keep them updated with the latest information about your business without going overboard. Facebook marketing provides you with an opportunity for connecting with your clients and prospective customers as well, so make the most of it.

ENCOURAGE YOUR ENTIRE WORKFORCE TO USE THIS PLATFORM

This is a really good resource for employee advocacy. You can reach out to the audience of your employees if you can provide your employees with content that is shareable. This will enable you to tap into their follower's base as well. It will help in increasing the reach of your business; however, the main issue that most marketers face will have to find ideal content. Also, either the employees are too willing or too scared of sharing the company's content on social media. You must start with an employee advocacy program that will allow your staff to make use of the really big networks like Facebook for sharing information about the business. Make use of Facebook as a promotional tool for showing off the various perks offered by the business, any new openings, and the work environment and so on. Make use of your workforce and encourage them to promote your business on social media platforms.

TRACKING AND ANALYZING YOUR MARKETING STRATEGY

If you want your Facebook marketing strategy to be successful, then, in such a case, you need to make sure that it is being analyzed regularly. There are different advertising metrics that you can make use of for this purpose. If you want to make some changes to your strategy or improve it, then you can obtain useful information from the Facebook analytics tools. Every marketer using social media will know about these tools. There are different free and paid applications that you can make use for gauging the effectiveness of your strategy. You will need insights into what works and doesn't for developing a strategy that will work. This is where Facebook Insights comes into the picture. This will help you in understanding what strategy is working, the kind of content that engages your audience, their likes and preferences, and so on.

OPTIMIZATION OF THE FACEBOOK PAGE

Your Facebook page is the starting point for all your efforts related to Facebook marketing. It will be ideal if it is ranked in Google, as well as Facebook, so that your customers and prospects can easily search for your brand name and find it with ease as well. Once they have found your page, it needs to be appealing for people so that they will want to 'like' it. Here are a few things that can be done for the sake of optimizing your page for the above-mentioned purposes.

Select a username that is descriptive and memorable: A URL of this sort is referred to as a vanity URL. The web address for your Facebook page will be your username for your Facebook page (for instance, www.facebook.com/nameofyourbusiness).   Most pages will be given a default URL comprising of numbers. Your username must be such that it can convey the topic of your page, or the name of your full business, so that it will be easy for the search engines, as well as customers, for finding your business in Google and Facebook searches. You will need to have at least 25 'likes' in order to claim this vanity URL.

Using descriptive keywords in the "About" section: The "about" section of your Facebook page is considered to be the primary source of the text-based real estate that you hold. Make sure that the description of your business, as well as your products, is as accurate as it can be, and make use of keywords that users might make use of while searching their queries. You must always include the URL of your website in the description that you provide, and this will encourage the users to click on it.

Use the appropriate category for your business: More often than not, businesses tend to list themselves in the wrong category. By doing this, they reduce their chances of showing up in the Facebook Graph Search. If you happen to be a local business, then you need to make sure that you properly select the proper category within which your business will fall. Only if you do this, will people be allowed to "check-in" at your business. If you don't have walk-in traffic, and you don't have a need for any check-ins, then, in such a case, you can select the option of Companies and Organizations.

Optimizing the images on your page: The first thing that a user visiting your page will see is your cover photo and your profile photo. The images that you use need to be of good quality, and must represent the feel and the look your brand wishes to exude. The images used must be according to the optimal size requirements. This means that the cover photo needs to be about 851 X 315 pixels and the profile picture must be 160 X 1160 pixels. Avoid images that are grainy, or are of a low quality.

Pinned Posts: Regardless of what you like to believe, most users will only visit your page once. They will interact with your page via the posts that show up on their newsfeed, but they wouldn't really go back and revisit your page. For this particular reason, the main function of your page is to make the user click on the 'like' button. Facebook allows the admin of a page to pin 1 post to the top of their page. Make sure that the topic of this one post that can be pinned is interesting, unique, and will grab the attention of the viewer.

USE FACEBOOK GROUPS

The primary tool that all businesses must use on Facebook for marketing their businesses are Facebook pages, but even groups can prove to be an effective marketing strategy in different industries and niches. When made use of in the right manner, groups can help in generating a lot of traffic, and can even lead to an increase in the engagement for your business. By taking a part in other industry-specific groups, establish yourself as an authority in that concerned field. Providing helpful advice and useful information will help you in becoming a valued member in any group and, once people start trusting you, they will want to learn more about you and your business. Perhaps one of the most important uses of a Facebook group will be the creation of, and participation in, groups that are related to your own area of interest. Groups will provide you with the opportunity for engaging with your audience in a manner that is personal, as well as relatable. It will also help your business in becoming a part of the regular conversations that your target audience have. Create a group that will be receptive of anything that is related to your field or industry. For instance, if you happen to be a contractor, then one viable idea will be to create a group on Facebook where people will be allowed to ask questions or discuss renovations, DIY building projects, and so much more.

ENCOURAGING SOCIAL SHARING ON FACEBOOK

Your business website and Facebook will need to work together and must have a symbiotic relationship. Your marketing funnel will help in directing traffic from your Facebook page towards your blog or your website; however, you will also need to make sure that you are providing the visitors of your site with an option of liking and sharing it on Facebook, and also for interacting with your page. Make sure that all the content on your site has a button for 'liking and sharing' right next to it. These buttons can be added manually, or you can also make use of different third-party services, such as AddThis or even WordPress plugin for customizing your buttons, and for making the process of adding them to your site easier. To give the visitors of your website an opportunity to like and interact with your page, you must include a page plugin towards the sidebar present on your site. When you are setting up the plugin, you will be provided with various options regarding the manner in which you want it to look. You can also include something like "Show Page Posts" so that the visitors to your website will be provided with a preview of the kind of content that is being typically shared on your webpage.

INCREASING THE VISIBILITY OF YOUR POSTS

One common complaint from most of the page owners is that most of their followers never really get to see their posts. This concern has been addressed by Facebook and they have managed to trace it down to two main factors. The first one is the sheer volume of content that is shared on Facebook; this means that there isn't sufficient space on the user's newsfeed for showing every single post. This will mean that the competition for the placement of the post within a user's newsfeed is quite fierce, and results in reduced exposure of organic posts. The second reason for the reduction in the post's visibility is that the algorithm of Facebook has been designed in such a manner that it will only show the content that is most relevant to its users. Now, relevancy is determined by taking into consideration a multitude of factors that include the manner in which a person has interacted with the page in the past, the kind of posts that are being shared, and also the popularity of the previous posts on a page amongst its users. To put it simply, the more popular your posts tend to be, their visibility will increase. You will be able to improve the visibility of your posts on the fan's feeds, and this will be by making use of the following tips:

Making use of videos in your posting strategy: The reach of videos is comparatively higher than that of text-only statuses. Videos are more attractive and they can help in capturing the attention of a viewer quite easily.

Take into consideration the page Insights for figuring out the kind of content that seems appealing to your audience: Page Insights usually consist of a lot of data about the kind of content that is able to achieve a higher rate of engagement with your audience. Check the formats of those posts that get the most visibility (whether they are images, videos, links, or texts), and also the topics that seem to be attracting your audience. Also, keep a track of the days and times, as well as the frequency of posting, that seem to work really well with your audience.

When posting about content that is promotional, make sure that you have included a relevant and entertaining backstory for ensuring optimal visibility. In 2014, it was announced by Facebook that they will be limiting the visibility of posts that were considered to be "too promotional" (this will include all those posts that will push a user to buy a product, enter into a contest, or where content has been reused from an ad).

To give your promotional posts the best shot at being seen, you will need to ensure that the content being provided is engaging, and it is more than just a plea for buying your product or visiting your website. Ask yourself this question "Will my fans think this post is interesting to read and interact with, even if they aren't interested in buying the product I'm offering?"

WHEN AND HOW OFTEN TO POST

Some business owners tend to get stuck up on posting at the correct time, and on the right day, for achieving optimal reach as well as engagement. The truth is that there isn't one fixed approach regarding the approach to post timing that will fit the needs of all users. There might be some research available online about the same; however, it will be better if you can do your own research. Make sure that you are consulting your Facebook Insights for making sure whether these practices will hold true to your audience as well. Some people tend to believe that posting on Thursday's and Friday's results in a higher rate of engagement, and then there are others who believe that posting between 1 pm and 3 pm helps in obtaining maximum visibility. Well, you can test these two theories out for yourself.

When it comes to the frequency of posting, there is one suggestion that drives the point home really well, and it is that you must know the difference and maintain a balance between being informative and annoying. There are some businesses that have managed to achieve success by posting between 5 to 10 times in a day, and then there are some that maybe post just 1 to 3 posts in a week and they have found that to be effective as well. Well, it was found by SocialBakers that posting less than 2 posts in a week will not help you in engaging with your audience and you might, in fact, actually lose engagement with them. If you end up posting more than 2 posts per day, then you will be bombarding your audience with too much information, so the ideal number of posts that you must post in a week will be between 5 to 10. This will help in ensuring maximum engagement.

EXPLORE PAID OPTIONS

It is quite possible to create decent visibility for your posts by making use of free strategies; you must look for ways in which you can supplement these organic strategies with a few paid ones. At present,

Facebook has got two main ways of extending the reach of your posts. The first one is by post boosts. This will help in improving the visibility of your post on the newsfeed of your user. You get to select if you will want your post to be shown to the followers of your page, friends of your fans, or others whom you get to select via targeting. Targeting options that are available for your post will include the interests, age group, gender, and location of your ideal audience. For boosting a particular post, you need to click on "Boost" when you are creating a new post. You will also find this option on any old posts if you are interested in boosting a post that has been published already.

Boosting posts is a really easy and efficient manner in which the reach of your posts can be extended; however, a better strategy is to opt for creating a promoted post. The second way in which you can use paid options will be by promoted posts. These can be accessed via the Facebook Ads Manager. For creating your own promoted post, you need to open the Facebook Ad Creator and click on the "Boost your posts" option. Even though it is referred to as Boosting, this does help with targeting and budgeting options in a better way than just the "boost" option present on the page.

WHEN TO PROMOTE A PARTICULAR POST

One of the major difficulties that business owners or marketers on Facebook face, is they understand when they are supposed to promote a post. Generally, your aim is to promote those posts that will help you in achieving a particular goal, like directing the traffic to your website, or for selling a particular product. When you have decided on the post that you want to promote, then you must consider using the STIR strategy. This strategy enables you to answer certain questions before you consider promoting a post. STIR strategy stands for Shelf life, Timing, Impact, and Results. Once you have managed to answer these questions without any bias, then you will understand whether you must promote such a post or not.

CHAPTER FIVE: FACEBOOK ADVERTISING

The psychology of the Facebook ad depends on how effective the ad is. There are different ways in which psychology can play a part in a FB ad. Use faces to capture the attention of the audience and make the ads personable. Emotions always win over rationality. Faces show expressions and expressions appeal to humans in general. Positive emotions lead to a better response to an ad. Bright colors always catch the viewer's attention, so use bright colors in the ad. Ads that promote cognitive dissonance appeal to an audience and so does exclusivity. You will learn about all this and much more in this section about creating and optimizing FB ads.

Facebook tends to offer various options for advertising, apart from having to promote a single post. You get to select the type of the ad based on various objectives. As has been mentioned previously, one of these objectives can be the boosting or the promoting of a particular post. There are different options that include promoting your page, directing others to your website, increase the rate of conversions, and also getting the users to claim any offer you have provided. Once you have selected the objective of your campaign, then you get to select your targeting options, budgeting options, and select the creative you want for your ad. Selecting the objective for your campaign can assist you in meeting your advertising goals. There are three placement options that are available for you, and these are your desktop newsfeed, mobile newsfeed, and the column on the right. The default option is that all these options will be selected. For stopping your ad from being displayed in any or all of these locations, you simply have to click on the "remove" option that is present beside the location name.

It is indeed quite easy to spend a lot of time and money on your Facebook ads without being able to achieve the objectives that you have set for yourself. Ads are an effective way of getting traffic, likes, and conversions; however, there are certain practices that are quite effective and will help you in achieving your goals in a relatively easier manner.

CREATING AND OPTIMIZING ADS

In this section, you will learn about the different steps that you need to follow to create and optimize Facebook ads.

APPROPRIATE EDITOR

There are two different tools that Facebook offers to create ads, and they are Ads Manager and Power Editor. When you try to decide between these two, you need to consider the size of your brand, or your business, and the number of ads that you want to run in one go. The Ads Manager suits the needs of most businesses, but the Power Editor is a good option for large advertisers who want to have precise control over various campaigns.

OBJECTIVE

Like various other social media networks, Facebook's Ad Manager helps design a campaign but, for that, you need to have an objective in mind. Before you start to design a campaign, the Ads Manager will ask you to select the objective of the campaign. There are ten different objectives that you can choose from. The list of objectives includes Page Post engagement, Website conversions, event responses, click to website, offer claims, App installations, Page Likes, App engagement, video views, and local awareness. When you select an objective, you give Facebook a better idea of what you want so that it can help them create an ad that suits your needs.

If your goal is to increase the traffic to your website, then select this option from the list of goals. Once you do this, Facebook will prompt you to type the URL that you want to promote. If you plan on using any automated marketing software, then you need to make sure that you are using a distinctive tracking URL that has UTM factors to track the traffic and the conversions.

SELECT YOUR AUDIENCE

If this is the first time using ads on Facebook, then you might need to test with a couple of various targeting alternatives until you find one that reaches your target audience. There are different targeting criteria that you can use. If you aren't sure if you need to select a specific or a broad audience, then you need to consider your objective to decide. If you want to drive traffic, then you need to focus on the type of people who will be interested in what you offer. If you want to build awareness about your brand or business, then it makes sense to create an ad that will appeal to a general audience. The different factors that you need to consider when you want to create an ad are location, age, gender, language, relationship, work, finances, ethnicity, life events, education, interests, behavior and connections. You have the option to select a custom audience as well. When you opt for a custom audience, then you can target people from your business's contact list, those who visit the website, or your app users. Once you find a group that will respond favorably to the ad, then you need to save the selected group of audience for further use later on.

Budget

Facebook offers two types of budgets for an ad, and they are a daily budget and a lifetime budget. If you want the ad to run continuously throughout the day, then you need to opt for the daily budget. When you use this option, Facebook will budget the pace of your expenditure each day. The minimum budget that you can set is 1 USD per day, and it needs to be at least twice your CPC. If you want to run the ad for a specific period, then you need to select the lifetime option. It means that Facebook will pace your budget over a period for which you want the ad to run. There are a couple of advanced options that you can use to specify your budgeting.

You need to decide the schedule for the ad. For instance, do you want the ad to run immediately, or do you want to customize the duration of the campaign? You can even customize the ad so that it runs for only specific hours of the day or days.

You need to select whether you want to bid for your objective, clicks and impressions or not. This decision will alter the way the ad will be displayed. When you do this, you will pay for a specific ad that will be shown to people within your targeted audience who are more likely to take the desired action. When you use Facebook Ads, Facebook will control your maximum bid. Opt for manual bidding when you don't want Facebook to bid for you. This option will give you complete control over the amount you want to spend per action that's completed. You also need to select the delivery option. The two delivery options that you need to choose from are standard and accelerated delivery. If you opt for standard delivery, then your ad will be shown throughout the day and, with accelerated delivery, you can reach your target audience quickly if it is a time-sensitive ad. The option of accelerated delivery requires manual bid pricing.

CREATE THE AD

What do you want the final ad to look like? The answer to this question depends on your objective. If you want to drive traffic to your website, then the Ad Manager will recommend the "Click to Website" advertisement option. This option is further divided into two formats and they are Links and Carousels. It means that you can either display a single-image ad

71

with Links or a multi-image ad with Carousel. After you choose the ad format, upload your creative resources. It is critical to note that there are certain specifications that you need to adhere to when you upload your creative assets. For instance, for a single-image ad, the text you use needs to be within 90 characters, the link title of 25 characters, the image ratio is 1.9:1 and the image size needs to be 1200 pixels X 627 pixels. If you want the images to appear in the newsfeed, then the suggested image width must at least be 600 pixels.

If you want to opt for a Carousel ad, then the recommended image size needs to be 600 X 600 pixels, the image ratio needs to be 1:1, the text cannot exceed 90 characters, the headline needs to be within 40 characters, the link description needs to consist of 20 characters, and the images you use cannot include more than 20% text.

REPORT

Once the ad is up and running, your work doesn't end there. You need to keep an eye on the performance of the ad. You can either use marketing software or the Facebook Ad Manager to view the results of the performance. If you decide to use Facebook Ad's Manager, then the sophisticated dashboard it provides will help give you an overview of the ad campaign. The dashboard emphasizes on an estimate of the costs that you incur per day; it is organized into columns that make it quite easy to filter through the ads so that you can create a custom view of the results. The key metrics that you need to look out for include performance, engagement, videos, website, apps, events, clicks and settings. The different Facebook advertising tools that you can use include the Facebook Ads Manager, Facebook Ads Manager App, Hootsuite Ads, Qwaya, AdEspresso, AdSpring, PerfectAudience, AdRoll and Driftrock.

ALWAYS USE AUDIENCE TARGETING

Advertising to the general audience without any form of targeting is a tedious job and you are setting yourself up for failure. Not just that, it will also be a waste of your time and money. Boosting a post from your page can be quite effective at times; however, taking the time for promoting a post within your Ad Manager can be quite effective, and it will help you in reaching your goals quite quickly. There are plenty of targeting options, and one thing that you must certainly try will be the option of targeting the audience according to their behavior.

CONTENT PLACEMENT

It is likely that most of the users will only take a look at the content that is placed at the beginning of your ad. For this reason, it is quite important that the content that you think is important needs to be placed right at the beginning of your ad. It can be a link or it can be a call to action.

ROTATING THE AD

If you are making use of specific targeting for your advertisement, you will have to keep advertising to a small audience over and over again. This will mean that you will have to change the image used for your ad after every week or two. Making use of the same content repeatedly will tire your customers and will reduce the chances of your ad getting noticed. It is very likely that your target audience will simply skip your ad. You can use conversions of pixels to track the effectiveness of your ads. If you are interested in purchasing multiple ads, then you must use conversion pixels for figuring out those ads that will help you in meeting your goals. You get to select from a range of conversion types while creating your pixel; this will include checkouts, registrations, page views generated, leads, and so on. More information about this can be found on the Help page on Facebook.

Using a strong call to action: You must always let the users know what is it that you want them to do. You needn't always be directive. Instead of telling them they must do something, tell them why they need to do this. This strategy is more convincing.

USE DIFFERENT ADS FOR DIFFERENT PLACEMENTS

Facebook allows you to use the same images and copy for different ads. It is quite important that the ads created were created while keeping the different platforms in mind. Ads displayed in the newsfeed on a phone, desktop, and the right column of the desktop are quite different, and these differences need to be taken into account.

Facebook is a brilliant platform for not just finding your target audience, but for engaging with them as well. When made use of in a proper manner, it can help you in increasing the flow of traffic, your visibility, as well as the rate of conversions.

SPLIT TESTING

Split testing helps to gauge the effectiveness of an ad and you can discover which ad, image or format helps drive better results. Split testing provides results based on statistics.

If you want to split test a Facebook ad creative, you need to select the Split Test option at the campaign level when you select your objective for the ad campaign. The only two objectives or which split testing isn't available yet are brand awareness and store visits. The split test feature allows you to test the audience, placement and bidding optimization.

From the Ads Manager dashboard, click on 'create' option. You can use Guided Creation instead of the Quick Creation flow, if you are using split testing for the first time.

Let us take an example to understand how split testing works. For instance, you have two ad formats and aren't sure which one to choose. Then you need to use split testing. The objective that you want to test is Traffic to target all those who have watched the content and need to be driven to the concerned website. You need to check the objective from the list given in the split test checkbox.

Once you select the objective, go to Ad Set level and from the Variable section click on Creative. It allows you to create two ad options- A and B. You can add up to 5 different ads at once if you select Test Another Ad.

Select your audience, placement, bidding optimization, schedule and test budget from the rest of the Ad Set.

In the previous example, the idea was to target all those who viewed the video content. So, in the audience section, you need to select Video custom audiences. Alternatively, you can also opt for Page Engagement or Website traffic. If you don't have any custom audience available, select 'Saved audience' and 'Lookalike audience.'

The next parameters you need to select are placement, delivery and optimization settings. You can opt for the default automatic placement option and optimize for Link Clicks (the other alternative is to optimize for Landing Page Views).

After this, you need to select the budget and the test schedule. You can run the test from anywhere between 3 to 14 days. Once you complete the Ad Set section, click on Continue to go to the Ad level.

Now, you need to create al the ad variations that you want to test. For instance, if you want to test the effectiveness of a carousel ad and a single image ad-you need to name Ad A as Carousel ad. Then you need to select the Facebook page in the Identify section.

Next, you need to select the carousel format and complete the ad. It means you need to ad images, headlines and links as well as descriptions.

Once you create the Ad A, it is time to move onto Ad B. To do this, click on Continue to Ad B. Facebook will automatically fill out the details according to Ad A. You need to change a couple of details to run the test. In the given instance, you need to change the ad format.

Since Ad A is a carousel ad, Ad B will be a Single Image ad. So, select the Single Image option from the ad format section and then add the image you used in your first carousel. Add the text, link, CTA (if any) and all the details you add here must match a card from the carousel ad you created.

Once you do this, click on Confirm and you can review the campaign. Now, you can successfully split test your ad.

You can use the creative split test option to compare two ad formats. Apart from this, you can also use it to test ad copy variation, headlines, call-to-action buttons, images, image-based carousel ads with video-based carousel ads and video ads against other video ads.

The split test option allows you to test different creative variables to make the most of your FB ads.

CHAPTER SIX: FACEBOOK STORIES

If you want to share your adventures with all your friends and followers on Facebook, then you need to use Facebook Stories. It is better than uploading an image and offers a couple of different options to jazz up the photos or videos you want to share. It is important to make sure that your ad campaign keeps up with all the latest updates and features on Facebook.

Facebook Stories is quite similar to the newsfeed, but the one difference between the two is that the former is more visual. It allows the user to add to different filters and effects to the camera, and requires you to post it in the Stories section and not upload it like a regular post. The stories that you create on Facebook can be shared with a group of people, or even a single user. Once you post a story, it will be available for 24 hours and then it disappears. It is quite similar to Snapchat Stories.

To make your photos ready for Facebook Stories, there are three options available to you. Open the Facebook app on your mobile, tap on the Your Story icon and then tap the Camera icon towards the top left side of the screen. You need to then press the record button to take a photo or a video. If you want to share a pre-existing photo, then you can upload it from your camera roll.

If you want to use this feature on the desktop, then you need to create a post like you normally will for any post for the newsfeed. Once it is ready, instead of uploading it like a usual post, you need to add it to your story.

Facebook introduced the Facebook Story feature in 2017. If you want your brand or business to feel hip and cool, then you need to make sure that you keep up with all the new developments that they keep introducing.

Facebook Stories' Practices for Businesses

The Facebook Story feature is a clone of the Snapchat Story option or the Instagram Stories feature. You need to make sure that you are familiar with this practice before you decide to use it on your business page. The first thing that you need to do is a pre-trip survey, check all the various buttons and their functions and then take it for a quick test drive.

As a business owner, you are the ambassador for your business and your Facebook post needs to reflect the same. Not just your posts, but your stories as well. You need to make sure that the emojis, filters, colors, frames, text colors and hashtags that you use are brand-oriented. Try to showcase your brand voice in a fun and a creative way.

You need to post Facebook Stories regularly and frequently. Facebook Stories provides a quick sneak peek into all that is going on with you and your business, so if you want to provide your followers and friends with entertaining updates, then opt for Facebook Stories. You need to take into consideration the time at which most of your followers will be online and then post it accordingly. You can also add to the story at any given point of time. You need to make sure that the content that you upload reaches your target audience; if it doesn't, then it defeats the purpose of advertising altogether.

Remember that all the followers of your business page will view the stories. For most people, stories are a simple way to form a personal connection with the viewers, so keep in mind that it is all about forming a personal connection without overburdening them with business clutter. You need to strike the perfect balance between business and a personal connection. Share some posts that are fun or light, and squeeze in some posts about business.

Your Facebook followers are always looking for something that is real and authentic. You are the ambassador for your business, but don't forget to provide your audience with something that will get them hooked. You can nurture and improve your relationship with your online users with Facebook Stories. To make the stories feel a little personal, you can add selfies, post images about the interesting bits of the day, offer a quick look into the operations, or you can even add some quotes or "deep thoughts." For instance, if you have a big announcement to make, or a big event planned for the future, you can use Facebook Stories to provide daily updates about the same.

The one thing that you must never forget when you are using Facebook advertising is that people head to Facebook because it is fun and entertaining for them, so you need to make sure that your Facebook Stories follows these simple criteria. The best way in which you can get people to look forward to your updates is to offer them something of value. You need to entertain them, share things that give them a feel of being valued, offer them insights that they can't get from anyone else, and showcase a private side of your business exclusively through your Facebook Stories.

Now that you know about Facebook Stories, the next step is to successfully incorporate them into your ad campaign.

Chapter Seven: Facebook Live

These days, live videos have become a rather popular form of advertising. Facebook Live is a live-video-streaming option that Facebook offers. You can broadcast a live video to your audience either through your business's profile or your personal profile. Facebook Live was introduced in April 2016 and it has become quite popular with online marketers and advertisers these days. Once you create a Facebook Live video, it will stay on your page or your profile so that all those who missed the live event can still view it. The video will show up on the newsfeed of a user during the event, and also when the event ends. You might wonder why a business needs to use this feature. Well, here are a couple of reasons that will certainly make you include Facebook Live videos into your ad campaign.

It helps the business connect with its audience in a genuine manner, and lends a human-like feel to the brand. If you ever felt that the audience tends to view your brand as a corporate robot, then you can change it with this feature.

You can easily interact with your users in real time and answer their questions. It gives you the opportunity to engage with your viewers when they are interested.

You can use Facebook Live to showcase an event to all those who cannot attend it in reality. It helps you connect with your customers and followers. It also helps you share any industry-related updates. Apart from this, it also helps you show off your business culture. It is the perfect way to lend a human feel to your brand.

WHEN TO USE FACEBOOK LIVE

You need to know when you can use Facebook Live. There are certain instances where a Facebook Live video works better than a regular post. In this section, you will learn about the different instances wherein you can use Facebook Live.

If you want to give your audience a taste of your business or brand's experience, then use Facebook Live. It works exceptionally if you have a physical storefront. It conveys the look and feels of your store or business that you cannot convey via texts or images.

Use this feature whenever you want to host any events or webinars. A well-planned webinar is an easy way to attract potential customers.

If you want to conduct any Q&A sessions, then what is better than doing it in real time? When you can interact with your viewers in real time, it has a better impact than regular online text conversations. In fact, if you schedule a Q&A session and promote it, then you can attract a lot of your viewers. It helps build a better relationship.

Use Facebook Live to offer online classes. Information is the most valuable commodity these days. If you can offer free and valuable information, you can develop a loyal audience base. The audience will want to visit your page more often if you can offer them something of value.

Product launches are quite exciting. If you are planning a product launch, then don't forget to stream it on Facebook Live. It is also a good platform to offer customer service.

HOW TO START A FACEBOOK LIVE EVENT

Well, now that you know what Facebook Live is about, the next step is to start using Facebook Live. In this section, you will learn about the simple steps that you need to follow to get started. You need a mobile phone or a desktop with a good camera and a microphone to start a Facebook Live event.

The first step is to click on the Live Video button. If you are using Facebook on your mobile phone, then a small button appears when you draft a post that says, "Live Video." Click on it to get started. If you are using a desktop, then you will see the "Live Video" option below the "Post" box.

The next step is to write an eye-catching description. The description, along with the video thumbnail, is the most important bits of the video. Without compelling content, you cannot entice the viewers to view the video. When writing the copy, make sure that it is direct, actionable, as well as informative. Try to give the viewer the information they need, but hold back some content to create a sense of curiosity.

Once you do all this, it is time to get in position and "Go Live." If you want to film a recurring series, then try to be consistent in your location. You need to use the same "set" if it is a recurring series, so choose the location carefully. Use an external microphone to improve the quality of the sound.

Once you are done, click on Finish and the stream ends. Make sure that you sign-off properly and don't just abruptly end the stream.

Once the Live stream ends, your video can still live on for all those viewers who missed the live event. You can share the video on the page, and even make any necessary edits to it.

USING FACEBOOK LIVE WITH A DESKTOP COMPUTER

If you want to use Facebook Live on the desktop, then you need to open a browser of your choice and then visit Facebook.com.

Click on the status text box present on the screen and then click on "Live Video."

Enter a brief description for the live video, select your privacy setting and then click next. When prompted, click on "Allow" to give Facebook the necessary permissions to access the webcam and the microphone. Once you do all this, you need to click on "Go Live" and the live feed starts.

BEFORE, DURING AND AFTER FACEBOOK LIVE

There are a couple of things that you need to do before, during and after a Facebook Live post.

The first thing that you need to do is promote before you broadcast a live video. It is important to understand that a live video is a lot like an event and not a blog post. You can always follow up the content that you post with consistent promotion, but, for a live video, the promotion comes before the actual event. In other words, you need to generate a sufficient buzz so that viewers watch the video. Well, Facebook allows you to target certain events and groups with your promotions. You need to push the upcoming announcement on your Facebook page as often as possible. It means that you need to share daily updates about the broadcast. You need to share something of value whenever you remind the audience about the event. Promote about the live event on all other social media handles of your business as well to attract a larger audience.

You need to limit all the distractions around you whenever you decide to use Facebook Live. Yes, Facebook Live is certainly more relaxed and offers a natural experience when compared to a regular advertisement, but it doesn't mean that you must not plan ahead. You need to remember that you represent the brand and, whatever you do on the live stream will reflect on your brand and business;

therefore, it is important that you always put your best foot forward.

You need to make some formatting decisions as well. How do you want to shoot the video, and when do you want to stream it? For instance, when you use the Facebook app on iOS, you have the option of posting the video horizontally or vertically according to your needs, so record a trial video to see which feature works the best for you.

Timing is crucial when it comes to a Facebook Live video. Send out email alerts, notifications, or even post about the upcoming event regularly on the page. Your aim is to reach your audience and engage them. If you schedule a live event pretty late or early in the morning, you will miss out on your viewers.

You need to continuously offer context to the viewers. You might think that it is sufficient to merely introduce yourself or your brand at the beginning of the video and stop after that. Don't work under the assumption that once a viewer clicks on the live video stream, they will stick around. Also, there might be other viewers who decide to join in later on. To engage all the viewers, you need to provide some context about the video at regular intervals.

You need to be responsive. Live comments and reactions make the experience engaging for the customer. You need to make the viewer feel like it is a two-way conversation so, for a conversation to be engaging, you need to interact with the viewers and respond to their comments or reactions.

You can also use this opportunity to announce a shout out.

CHAPTER EIGHT: FACEBOOK ANALYTICS

HOW TO REVIEW ENGAGEMENT

Now that you have worked quite hard to develop your audience base, the next step is to review your engagement on Facebook. In fact, Facebook will penalize you if the audience engagement decreases. It means that if the audience doesn't interact with your posts, then Facebook will steadily reduce the number of times your posts show up on the audience's newsfeed. A higher rate of engagement usually implies a growth in your audience base. If you want to review your engagement on Facebook, then the first step is to open the Insights page. Once you do this, then you need to select Posts. Scroll through the page and go to the section titled as "Your 5 Most Recent Posts" and click on the header to see a list of all your published posts. Now, use the drop-down menu on the right side and click on Engagement Rate.

The Engagement Rate is determined according to the number of comments, shares, clicks and likes your posts receive and is showed as a percentage of the total people a post reached. If the engagement rate is more than 1%, then it is good. The Engagement rate between 0.5% to 0.99% is average, and anything below 0.5% needs to be improved. You must take a detailed look at all your posts to understand the way your fans interact with the content you post. On the right-hand side, you will find different options like 'comments, shares and likes' and select them all from the drop-down menu. A 'like' is quite simple and requires less involvement from a user than 'shares and comments'; therefore, 'shares and comments' are weighed more heavily and reach more users. All this data will give you an insight into what works best for you and your audience. Once you have this data in hand, you can make the necessary changes to your marketing and advertising strategies.

BOOSTING POSTS

Facebook is one of the best social media resources to target your target audience. It gives businesses an access to a wide audience base. Facebook allows business owners and marketers alike to invest in a Facebook boost post. It is a post promotional tool that Facebook offers. A Facebook boost post is a post from your business page that will appear higher up on your target audience's newsfeeds. This tool that

Facebook offers comes at a fee. The fee payable depends on the number of people you want the post to reach. Simply put, the fee payable for a Facebook boost post is directly proportional to the number of the impressions that your post receives.

A boosted post is not the same as a sponsored post. A sponsored post is like ads wherein you can select your targeted demographic location and then invest accordingly to create awareness about your brand or business. You must opt for a Facebook boost post only after you run analytics about your target audience in a given geographical location. When you do this, you will have the necessary information about the target audience that you want to reach. Boosted posts will never get lost amongst other posts like birthday wishes or any other congratulatory posts. A Facebook boost post comes with a certain degree of guaranteed visibility as per your requirements. In fact, boosted posts enjoy a greater degree of visibility amongst those who liked your business page. Whenever anyone comments on, or 'likes' a boosted post, then it will automatically show up on the newsfeed of their friends; regardless of whether they are following your page or not. Thereby, a boosted post increases the online visibility of the brand or the business.

If you want to use a Facebook boost post, then the first thing that you need to know is the post that you want to boost. You can either boost a new Facebook post, or something that was already published and is still relevant for your conversions. The only condition is that any of the past posts you want to boost need to be published after 21st July 2012.

If you want to use this feature, then you need to be aware of the kind of audience that you want to reach. A boosted post will be automatically optimized for the newsfeeds of the users who like your page, along with their friends. The post you want to boost needs to be directed towards a specific audience according to their interest, age, gender and location. Once you are certain of the audience you want to reach, then you need to consider the budget that's necessary to boost that post. The budget will depend on the duration for which you want that particular post to stay boosted. The cost is directly proportional to the estimated audience to whom the post will be visible.

There are two simple steps that you need to follow if you want to boost a post. The first step is to establish a goal for the Facebook post. Some of the key objectives that you need to consider when you decide to boost a post are its reach, the followers, engagement and traffic. Once you have your objective in mind, the next step is to select the post you want to boost.

You can use the Facebook Ads Manager to boost a Facebook post. To do this, you need to go to the Facebook Ads Manager option, and click on the "+Create Campaign" option. Once you click on it, you will see a couple of different campaign objectives that you can choose from.

Select 'traffic' as the objective for driving more clicks to the link you share. If you want to boost a text or an image, then you can select 'engagement' or 'brand' awareness as your objective. Now, you need to select your audience, your budget and the devices that you want to use for your Facebook boost post. For the Facebook pages with a large following, you need to opt for 'Engaged People' as it will help you reach most of the active users of all those pages.

If your page doesn't have a large following, then you must opt for the Audience Tab. If you have Facebook pixel installed on your website, and your page has a little traffic, opt for the Lookalike Audience option (present under the Audience section). Once you select your target audience, you need to create the ad. Creating a new advertisement is quite similar to creating a Facebook post. If not, you can always boost an existing post and then you need to click on

Place Order. Once you do this, your order for boosting a post will be placed. If your ad is approved (approval takes about 30 minutes), then it will be boosted to your chosen audience.

Boosting a post is more effective than a regular Facebook ad in terms of the cost and its reach. When you boost a post through the Facebook Ads Manager, then the post will organically show up on the newsfeed of the followers of that page. If you want better results, then you need to convert a Facebook post into an ad. Boosting a post one day after you post the link will give Facebook sufficient time to measure its effectiveness.

Facebook Ads Manager, Hootsuite Ads and Facebook Exclusion Targeting are the best tools that you can use to boost Facebook posts. The Facebook Ads Manager is designed for small to medium-sized marketers, and it allows the user to create a boosted post from any existing post or from photos or images on your device. It helps marketers track the performance of the boosted posts, revise the ad budgets, edit an existing post and receive push notifications. Hootsuite Ads automatically generates Facebook ads, and creates boosted posts according to the existing organic Facebook page posts. It scans the Facebook page of your business, and enables you to zero in on the posts that you must boost. It also helps with an automated targeting and bidding algorithm that enables you to launch a boosted post. Facebook Exclusion Targeting is a tool that helps the user avoid targeting the same user twice. With the help of this tool, you can successfully exclude any of your existing customers from a boosted post, and helps generate new leads. This tool reduces your cost per action or cost per click. It also helps your boost post to reach all those people who are more likely to buy or convert and not just random users.

CAN YOU USE OTHER PROGRAMS?

An important part of a successful social media marketing and advertising campaign involves the monitoring of various metrics to analyze the performance of your posts. There are various Facebook analytics tools that you can use to analyze the necessary metrics. In this section, you will learn about the best Facebook analytics tools available.

FACEBOOK INSIGHTS

The first place that you can look at is Facebook itself. The Insights tool is available to the admin of your business page once the page has more than 30 followers. It provides detailed metrics about the post, and the engagement they receive. Audience analysis, along with a demographic and location breakdown, will help you understand your followers in a better manner. You can view the engagement metrics for each post. The breakdown of the 'likes' page into paid and organic sections helps you analyze the value of any promotional posts.

LikeAlyzer

It is a free tool that is easy to use. You can enter any Facebook page and then measure or analyze its performance. The tool grades a page out of 100 and then it compares the page with other similar pages. It means that you can get a preview of your competitor's pages as well. It gives you the necessary metrics and also some suggestions to make any changes. The metrics it provides includes the rate of engagement, timing and the length of the posts.

SimplyMeasured

There are four different Facebook reports that SimplyMeasured offers. The four reports it offers are Insights report, competitive analysis report, fan page report and content analysis. The Insights report it prepares repurposes the data that Facebook Insights provides into graphs. Information in this report includes reach, stories, post type, follower statistics, activity, demographics, page likes, impressions and engagement. The competitive analysis helps you compare 10 different fan pages up to 250k fans. It shows the overall comparative metrics in the form of charts. The fan page report gives details of the content metrics, metrics related to the community and the engagement. The top users are classified according to the number of posts, comments and total engagement. The content analysis report analyses the breakdown of the content you share - types of post, its engagement and common keywords.

SOCIOGRAPH.IO

Once you receive the authorization, you can use this tool to analyze any Facebook fan page for free. It displays the total number of posts, commenters, likers and the authors. It displays the average number of likes, shares and comments that every post receives, the different types of post, and the top posts within a given timeline. You can go all the way back to the posts since the page was created. It doesn't provide a lot of actionable data, but it is easy to use.

AGROPULSE

It offers two Facebook tools free of cost. The first Facebook tool allows you to benchmark your page and helps you understand whether the content's performance is above average and the metrics you need to focus on. The second tool allows you to host competitions, quizzes and sweepstakes on your Facebook timeline. It also tracks your response rate and the time taken to reply. This tool includes the most influential users and the users who mention your brand the most. The detailed reports it provides include page-level and timeline-level analytics. You can see the detailed breakdown of your brand's organic, paid and viral reach on Facebook. It helps you understand the kind of content that works best for you. It also offers an ROI (Return on Investment) calculator that you can use to determine your Facebook marketing and advertising budget. It has the option of customizing the reports and you can download them in the form of a 20-slide PowerPoint presentation.

QUINTLY

It is a really powerful tool that can be made use of for obtaining really detailed analytics of social media and helps you keep a track of your business on social media platforms such as Facebook, Twitter, YouTube, Google+, LinkedIn and Instagram as well. Quintly also helps you in benchmarking those features that help you compare your performance with that of your competitors in the industry, and also against the industry averages. The Quintly dashboard also offers customization so you can simply focus on the stats that matter more to you when compared to the rest.

CHAPTER NINE: BEST PRACTICES

FACEBOOK RESOURCES

There are a few difficulties that marketers tend to run into while marketing on Facebook. Low familiarity with the platforms happens to be quite a common challenge. Facebook is quite simple to use, and you certainly don't need to be a rocket scientist to figure things out on this platform. There are different researches, as well as management tools that are available, and people don't use them due to their lack of awareness. This prevents them from making the most of the features that this platform has got to offer. The process of creating ads manually can cause a slight inconvenience. Even if you have a really good idea, developing an individual advert on this platform is time-consuming. It is quite a big investment, especially for small businesses. If you aren't well acquainted with the world of social media, then, in such a case, Facebook marketing might be slightly difficult to learn. There are plenty of tutorials and articles helping with Facebook advertising, but this can be tricky to master and, without the right resources, you might just end up wasting your time. Finally, the third major obstacle that most of the newbies to the world of Facebook marketing find is that they get carried away by superficial numbers like the total 'likes' or views that they have received. These metrics must not be your sole focus. Your major concern needs to be the ROI (Return on Investment). With the right set of tools and some knowledge, it can be calculated quite easily.

Well, these are minor obstacles that you might encounter; however, you needn't worry about them. There are third-party developers who have been working towards making the process of Facebook marketing easy for you. There are some tools that you must familiarize yourself with. These tools will help in overcoming, or avoiding these obstacles altogether. You will find a list of tools that will come in handy below.

When it comes to social media advertising and marketing, Facebook is amongst the best platforms available. If you want to use Facebook for advertising your business or brand, then you need to go through the list of Facebook resources discussed in this section.

FACEBOOK FOR BUSINESS

The first resource that you need is Facebook for Business. If this is your first attempt at using Facebook to promote your business, then the first page that you need to check is Facebook for Business. On this page, you will find useful information regarding the ways in which you can use Facebook to increase your sales, build brand awareness and check the latest updates and tools available.

ADVERTISER SUPPORT

Facebook is an amazing platform that helps you reach your target audience with highly targeted ad campaigns. To know where to start, you must visit the Advertiser Support page on Facebook. Any queries you have about advertising on Facebook will be answered on this page.

ADVERTISER EDUCATION

You need to visit the Advertiser Education page on Facebook if you want to gather more information about the ways in which Facebook can help your business become a success. You will find all the information that you need about Facebook pages, Facebook ads, best practices and much more. The Facebook Blueprint page has about 34 learning e-modules that you can use to gain some practical, as well as hands-on experience about the best practices and resources on Facebook. To access this page, all that you need is a Facebook account. You will even find certain online courses that are custom-made for your business.

VIDEO TUTORIALS

If you want to learn more about how it all works, then you need to visit the Facebook Video Tutorials page. This page includes various success stories and tutorials that will inspire you.

CREATIVE TOOLS AND TIPS

Facebook is quite popular with marketers and users alike. All this popularity has created a lot of clutter, and it poses a big challenge for any business. In other words, your ad needs to be creative and engaging if you want to attract your target audience; however, if you have a limited budget or limited resources, then how can you address this problem? The answer to this problem is quite simple; you need to visit the Facebook Creative Shop. This is your one-stop shop for all the different tools that

Facebook has developed that will improve the quality of your ads, and help you reach a wider audience base within a limited budget. The Facebook team continuously works with businesses to develop various tools, processes and creative ideas that will help the businesses grow.

GUIDE FOR ADVERTISERS

If you want any expert tips on how you can create brilliant ads on Facebook, then visit the Guide for Advertisers page on Facebook. In this page, you will find all the information that you need to develop Facebook ads that are impactful and powerful. Some of the topics included in here are the ways in which you can gain more conversions, accelerate the growth of your app and much more.

According to your objectives and the results you are looking for, the Facebook ads will differ. The Facebook Ads Guide will help you make sure that the Facebook ads you design will look their best.

ADVERTISING POLICIES

It is important that you are well versed with the advertising policies of Facebook. Before your ad is up and running and you can connect with your audience, the ad you design, or your ad campaign, needs to be in sync with the advertising policies of

Facebook. All the information that you need about this is available in the ad review process of Facebook. On this page, you will find a list of reasons that can disqualify your ad, along with a list of all the restricted content. Only when the ad complies with all these guidelines can you start the ad campaign.

HELP CENTER

If you have any queries about using Facebook for your business, then you can find the answers to those queries at the Help Center. You will get helpful information on topics like managing your password, reporting an issue and much more. Apart from this, if you have any particular questions, you can post the same on the Help Center page. The Facebook Help team and other Facebook users will answer your queries. You can also check the questions that other Facebook users post. You can visit the Help Center page if you come across any content that seems harmful or abusive. Apart from this, if you have any suggestions or feedback that you want to share with the team at Facebook, you can post the same at the Help Center page.

ADDITIONAL TOOLS

Flow: Driftrock develops this, and this is a tool that was designed for targeting your audience. It syncs with your existing e-Commerce platform and it will help in gathering customer data that will, in turn, help you in targeting the existing customer base that you have in a better and an accurate manner. You can either focus on your existing clients and mailing list, or you have the option of finding new people who have similar characteristics like your current customer base, and will help in unearthing new leads and prospects as well.

Google Analytics: This tool is mainly used for tracking web traffic. If you aren't making use of this in relation to your Facebook marketing campaign, then you are missing out on some good stuff. This tool allows you to view the links that directed different Facebook users towards your site, and their behavior once they go there. It is the perfect tool for determining your ROI, as well as the effectiveness of your website.

Real Geeks' Facebook Marketing Tool: This was developed while keeping real estate agents in perspective. This tool automatically syncs with different websites, gathers important information for the purpose of creating Facebook ads on the fly, and will save you all the time that you will have usually had to spend if you were to create an ad manually. It has got analytics functions to offer that users can use for judging those ads that are effective, and this will help you in coming up with future strategies that will suit your needs.

Agora Pulse: This tool provides you with an opportunity to link your Facebook, Twitter, Instagram, LinkedIn, and other social media accounts into a centralized location. You will be able to schedule and publish your posts, monitor your activity on these social media sites, engage with your customers, and even monitor your competition on the market.

Social Bakers: This is a social analytics tool that is capable of working along with any social media application that is available. This will help you with competitive research, provide you with insights of your audience, KPIs, and other data in the form of customized reports that can be tailor-made according to your goals.

DrumUp: This is an amalgamation of content marketing and social media tools that can help you in finding content that will be considered to be appropriate and effective by your audience. It helps in content research and recommendation, apart from providing you with insights about the social media strategy that you have opted for.

<u>ShortStack</u>: This tool is designed for making the process of the creation of ads and contests easier while using Facebook. The user interface of this app is quite simple, and it has got different tools within it that can help you in creating a campaign that will fit your needs.

Chapter Ten: Posting Quality Content

Evaluate Everything

There is only one way to determine if your efforts are working effectively, and that is to evaluate all of the data. Some social media platforms have tools built in to help you do this, and there are plenty of third-party options for analytic tools. Use these to look at what gets the most response in terms of the content you are sharing or promoting and, just as importantly, what isn't getting the level of response that you need. That way, you can figure what to drop and what to keep on doing.

Make Sure You Post at the Right Time

It isn't just what you are posting that has an effect of the numbers of people that see it, the amount that interacts with it and shares it. The timing of your posts is vital – most B2B businesses tend to stick posting during normal working hours but, even then, some days will elicit a far better response than others will. Do your homework – know when your target audience is likely to be online, and schedule your posts to go live when they are there.

BUILD YOUR CONNECTIONS

One of the most common mistakes that social media markets make is to talk at their audience, rather than to them. Talk to your followers, engage with them, and interact with them. They want to know that you are human, not just some computer churning out automatic responses. Ask them to share their thoughts and make sure that you respond to their comments in good time. If they send you messages, communicate with them straight away; effectively ignoring potential customers will simply drive them away.

GO VISUAL

Large blocks of text put off people, but they stop and take notice of images. Photos, videos and infographics have information in them that people tend to take in easier. Make sure your visual content is strong, appealing and relevant to your business.

MAKE EACH OF YOUR CHOSEN PLATFORMS UNIQUE

There are plenty of tools that allow you to share content across several platforms but, while this might work for information that is highly important, doing it for every piece will simply make all of your platforms identical. People that follow you on one platform are likely to follow you on all of them, and they do not want to see identical content – that will ensure they only follow you on one. Make each of your accounts unique, and that will draw more people in and gain you more followers and more potential customers.

MAKE IT WORTHWHILE FOR PEOPLE TO FOLLOW YOU

When someone follows you on a social media account, they want to feel some kind of appreciation for that. Offer up rewards for subscribing or following you – maybe a small discount on a product or entries into a prize draw. People need an incentive to join you, and it will keep them engaged and interested if they get something out of it.

BE A "PERSONABLE" PERSON

While social media may be a more relaxed manner of marketing your business, you do still need to maintain an air of professionalism. Yes, do give out some personal details that will give your business that human face, like a birthday or a bit of banter here and there, but never start giving out your personal views on things on your business page. If you start getting hot under the collar about politics or talking down the latest celebrity gaffe, you can very easily start to turn your followers away from you.

PLAN CAROUSEL ADS

Before you can launch a Facebook carousel ad, you need a plan and strategy for your ad campaign. Once you decide the message, image and the strategy you want to use, then creating the ad is quite easy. You need to think about your target audience, the action that you want them to perform and the content that will persuade your target audience to perform the action. You need to make a list of your customers and their interests, include trackable links to your website and include high-quality videos or images that are consistent with your message.

Before you can start, you need to check the recommended size of images and other information given in the Facebook Ads Guide page. You can look at different carousel ads format for some inspiration. You can then create a mockup of the same in the Creative Hub.

To create a carousel ad for your page, follow the following steps.

Click on the Promote button on the page → Get More Website Visitors

In the Ad Creative section present on the upper right side of the page, click on Edit.

Enter the desired URL that you want people to be directed to when they click on the ad. If you want each carousel card to send the visitor to a different URL, then you can edit the ad in Ads Manager.

Once you do this, add the Text for your ad.

Click the + sign, under the Images section to add carousel cards.

Click on the number of the card you want a particular image to be added to.

Then click on Upload image - to add an image from your computer or you can click on Select Image to upload an image from your library that you previously used.

Click on Reposition Image, if you want to crop the image.

You need to add a Headline for every card in the carousel.

Click on Ad Creative section and click on Save when you want to save the changes to the carousel.

Then you need to fill out the necessary information about the Audience, Budget and Duration along with Payment section to complete the ad. Then click on Promote.

USE POWER EDITOR TO CREATE CAROUSEL ADS

One of the most important benefits of using Power Editor to create a carousel ad is that you can add more text in the ads. In Ads Manager, you can use 25 characters for a headline and about 90 characters for any text. If you use Power Editor, you can add more text.

Once you Start your campaign and name the ad set and ad, you can configure the ad in Power Editor. You will notice that there aren't any limitations about text.

You can tell the audience the complete story about the subject with Power Editor.

You can also customize the display URL area. You can use this extra space to add some additional text about the product or provide them information about any deals. This feature comes in handy when the URL is long and bulky. For instance, you can use the extra tracking in the website URL and to make sure that people know where they are going, add the real website address in the Display URL box.

If you want to reinforce your call-to-action, you can use the Display URL area to highlight the Sign-up option.

In Power Editor, you have the option of tagging other pages in the text in an ad. It helps make the ad look like a regular post and also increases its visibility. Whenever you tag other pages, make sure that the tags are relevant. To tag another page or other people in the ad, you need to type @ followed by the name of the page or the person into the Text box and select the relevant name from the drop-down menu. If you are using organic content for the ad, then tagging increases the visibility.

There are two types of ads available in the Power Editor and they are product ads and carousel ads.

The carousel ads set up in Power Editor can display up to five products. You need to not only select the images to be displayed in the ad, but you can also add the link to a unique website for each of the products. Also, every ad in the carousel has a description and headline of its own.

For a carousel ad, the image size needs to be 600x600 pixels. Once you make all the necessary changes to the ad, your ad is ready to be displayed.

HAVE A SOCIAL MEDIA MANAGER

It might be seen as being a non-job, but it is amazing the results that a proper social media manager can obtain. Not everyone is proficient at social media and, if you are not, it is better to have someone at the helm that can converse with others, engage easily, like posts and share content easily. That way, you can get on with running your business and reap the rewards of a successful marketing campaign.

IF IT ISN'T WORKING, DITCH IT

Not everything is going to work; it doesn't matter how much analysis you do, how many new team members you recruit, there will be that one platform that simply isn't right for your business. If nothing is working, and you are not gaining any results from it, ditch it and walk away. There are better things for your time and energy to be used on.

Build Up Relationships with Businesses

If there are businesses that are in the same kind of sector as you, or the same industry, friend them and follow them, but only if they are not direct competition. You may be able to refer customers to each other, share followers and pick up tips. It might just surprise you how much good can come of this, so give it a go but don't friend or follow everyone indiscriminately – be choosy.

Face the Trolls

The more successful you become, the more attention your social media accounts will draw, and that means the inevitable abuse from some people. If you find that you have haters on your pages, be professional in your dealings with them. Choose carefully how to respond – sometimes it must be a polite response, other times, it works better to ignore them and, in some cases, you will need to block them. Do not block someone just because they don't like your company; that is not good business sense, and it doesn't send out a good message.

Don't Use it for Pitching a Hard Sell

Facebook is perceived as a domain where people can engage in some social activity, chat with their friends, check photos and videos posted by others, and simply relax. You will need to join in on a conversation and become a part of a community, instead of being the "outsider" who is trying to sell quite aggressively. There are certain hard-sell tactics that you must avoid. These include the use of advertising slogans, posting over and over again about a particular product or service, or providing excess information about a product or service not related to any conversation. Your followers might just unfollow you. What's worse? You might even attract a lot of negative comments about your business.

Always have a Clear Goal

It is quite important to have a clear goal in your mind while you use Facebook, and a well-defined strategy to achieve that goal. For instance, a coffee shop might just decide that its goal is to increase the sales that were generated via Facebook by 10% over a period of six months, and then their strategy can include the following:

- They can create a post daily that will feature a particular "special" of the day by making use of a coupon code so that the particular sale is capable of being tracked on Facebook.

- They can post a photo featuring a customer with a cup of coffee from their coffee shop.

- They can also encourage users to start posting their own photos (maybe while sitting at the coffee shop concerned, or with some coffee) to bring in more participation.

- Setting a goal, as well as a strategy, will help in providing you with direction and reaching the success that you wanted.

CREATING A HUMAN SIDE

In general, a user on Facebook will want to communicate with another person and not engage in a conversation with an impersonal business. Whoever is responsible for managing the Facebook page for a business or a brand must be capable of writing and developing content that will give a human "feel" to the page, and make it more likable and welcoming. Don't make things sound too formal or stiff.

POSTING REGULARLY

Unlike the other forms of media like television, magazines, newspapers, and so on, social media provides you with the option to include regular updates. Most of the Facebook users tend to check their pages at least once a day, and they will need to see that your business is posting some new content. Depending upon the manner in which your audience is receiving the information you are posting, you can decide when and how much to post.

ENCOURAGING COMMENTS

You must encourage Facebook users to respond to your posts, and to comment on your posts about your business or a topic that interests them. When a user does post something, make sure that their post is being replied to within 24 hours. Failure to reply can be perceived as lack of interest on your part and, if you aren't responding, the users might stop following you.

USE PICTURES AND VIDEOS

One of the most appealing elements of Facebook will be the fact that it allows users to post pictures and videos. This will help in keeping your audience engaged as well as entertaining. For instance, a clothing chain can perhaps post images of the new stock as soon as it arrives, or a personal trainer can post an instructional video providing instructions about how a particular exercise must and must not be done, and so on. Try to get as interactive as you possibly can, and engage your audience by hosting different contests, conducting surveys, creating offers, and so on. Facebook is supposed to be fun, so don't forget to include the "fun" element into your marketing strategies. Two of the most popular reasons why a user will follow a business page on Facebook are discounts and giveaways. Contests and games can be made use of for making your page exciting. Facebook can be used for conducting customer surveys. If you do want to conduct a survey, keep the questions simple and the survey short.

NURTURING THE RELATIONSHIP

It does take a while for establishing a good relationship with other Facebook users, so you will need to be patient. You must engage in conversations, provide meaningful content, and develop rewards for retaining existing followers and for attracting new customers.

DON'T FORGET TO USE FACEBOOK INSIGHTS

Facebook Insights can help you in understanding more about all those who like your page and choose to follow you. Once you are aware of the characteristics of those who are following you, then you can tailor your posts to meet their needs and keep them interested as well. For instance, if a bookstore that caters to customers of all age groups, but most of the followers happen to be between the ages of 18 to 25, then, in such a case, the offers offered by them on Facebook must be designed keeping in mind the kind of audience they have, whereas the offers that they provide in the store must be more diverse.

THE ENGAGEMENT PATTERN OF YOUR FOLLOWERS

Make sure that you are posting actively on Facebook according to the engagement pattern of your followers. When it seems that they are most likely to engage, that's when you need to post. This will take a while to get it right and spend some time trying to figure this out. It might not sound important, but it most certainly is. You will understand this when your followers grow and the "likes" on your posts increase.

TAGS ARE IMPORTANT

Tags are quite important. Yes, there are certain people who have clearly gone overboard with tagging; however, tags help the users to discover your content. Be judicious in your usage of tags.

Don't Forget the Commenters

Always remember to respond to any direct comments, opinions and questions. Let your followers know that their opinions matter and that someone is paying attention to them. This helps in lending a human touch to the Facebook page.

Make Sure Your Business Profile is Fully Completed

On your profile, you are given plenty of space to give your followers information about you. Leaving parts of it blank will not endear you to any of your followers; they want to know all about you, they want to know what makes you worth following and supporting. Blank spaces say that you are not interesting, and nobody will take the time to follow someone who can't even complete their profile.

Make Your Followers Want to See Your Updates

The ultimate goal of any marketing plan is to make people want to read your content. You want these people to be hanging on to every word you write, and to be eager to see the next installment. You want them to be checking constantly to see if you posted anything, and the only way to do this is with high quality, valuable, relevant content.

IF YOU SHARE SOMETHING, COMMENT ON IT

Don't just click on the button that lets you share something or retweet it; add a comment to it to tell people why you think the content is worth sharing, This helps you to build up your own expertise and a reputation for being that expert; that, in itself, adds a lot of value to whatever you are sharing.

CHECK YOUR GRAMMAR AND SPELLING

This is important. You are a professional businessperson and the worst thing you can do is publish content that is badly written and full of spelling errors. Check your work, double check it, and then check it again to make sure it is professionally written before you publish.

Never Post on the Hour

Most meetings and tasks are scheduled to start at the top of the hour so, when the clock strikes, people are moving on to the next item on their list, not looking at their social media accounts. If a task or meeting finishes early or overruns a bit, that gives a small window to check those accounts; therefore, it makes sense to post your content just before or just after the hour, not on it. This way, more people will see what you are posting.

Learn the Platform Guidelines

Familiarize yourself with the guidelines that each platform has, and make sure you know what is and isn't acceptable in terms of behavior and content. Common sense must dictate the kinds of content; you need to check up on the terms and conditions for the platform before you post it. Some, in particular, like Facebook, are constantly changing their guidelines on things like running competitions, and breaching those can result in a penalty, suspension or complete expulsion from a platform and that is not what you want for your business.

Make Sure Your Profile Includes Your Location

People need to know where your business is based, even if your service or product is Internet-based. If they know where you are, they can find you and check in, particularly on Facebook. This is more important if you have a physical store that people can visit – not adding your location can lose you a lot of potential customers.

CONCLUSION

I want to thank you once again for purchasing this book. I hope it proved to be an enjoyable and informative read.

Social media marketing is all the rage these days. The benefit that social media marketing offers over the traditional methods is quite impressive. Of all the different social networking platforms that are present, Facebook is the most popular of all. With over a billion active users, this is the best place to find your potential audience. Facebook not only has great potential, but its popularity is increasing as well. By learning how to make the most of this platform, you can design a marketing strategy that will help you in making the most of it. In this world where social networking rules our lives, businesses cannot afford to lag! Time, effort, and patience are the three key concepts for developing a successful Facebook advertising strategy!

Well, it is quite easy to use Facebook, isn't it? Facebook is a brilliant social media platform that can work wonders for your business and your brand. Now that you are armed with all the information that you need to optimally use Facebook advertising, all that you need to do is get started. Use all the simple tips, tricks and strategies given in this book to give your business a much-needed social media boost! So, what are you waiting for? Get started today!

Thank you and all the best!

RESOURCES

https://thrivehive.com/benefits-of-facebook-for-business/

https://viralsolutions.net/facebook-groups-10-lessons-learned-building-a-strong-community/

https://www.jonloomer.com/2013/07/11/increase-facebook-likes/

https://adespresso.com/blog/killer-strategies-improve-facebook-conversion-rate-practical-examples/

https://www.postplanner.com/boost-facebook-engagement-infographic/

https://blog.hubspot.com/marketing/facebook-paid-ad-checklisthttps://neilpatel.com/blog/11-facebook-advertising-tools-thatll-save-you-time-and-money/

http://home.bt.com/tech-gadgets/internet/social-media/facebook-stories-what-is-it-and-how-does-it-work-11364169985164

https://curatti.com/facebook-stories-best-practices/

https://sproutsocial.com/insights/facebook-live-tips/https://www.socialmediaexaminer.com/how-to-use-facebook-live-from-your-desktop-without-costly-software/

https://www.brandwatch.com/blog/8-free-facebook-analytics-tools/

https://www.digitalvidya.com/blog/facebook-boost-post/

https://thrivehive.com/how-to-check-engagement-on-facebook-instagram-and-twitter/

https://smallbiztrends.com/2015/12/facebook-business-resources.html

https://www.wordstream.com/blog/ws/2011/10/19/10-facebook-tips-for-content

INSTAGRAM MARKETING

WHAT THE TOP INFLUENCERS AND BRANDS KNOW THAT YOU DON'T ABOUT THE HOTTEST SOCIAL MEDIA

Chapter 1: Basics and Getting to Know Instagram

Introduction

In the 21st century, social media has become a trend in the communication industry with various platforms having been created. Instagram is one of the leading social media platforms that has become rampant in recent years. Actually, it has rapidly gained popularity because of everyone's obsession with mobile photography.

So, what exactly is Instagram? It is a social networking application created for sharing photos and videos from a smartphone. Similar to other renowned networking applications, anyone who creates an Instagram account has a profile and a news feed. Ideally, when you post a photo or video on Instagram, it gets displayed on the profile. Other Instagram users who follow you will see the new post in their own feed. Similarly, you get to see posts from other users that you are following on your feed.

Apart from using Instagram for posting photos and videos, a number of influencers and big brands are using the platform to make an impact on their marketing strategy. Instagram has been discovered as one of the best platforms that one can use to reach new audiences. In fact, it is a top rated performing channel for social action. Marketing through Instagram has been budded as Instagram Marketing. This mode of social media marketing is on the rise and many businesses have embraced it for a more successful marketing strategy.

A big reason why Instagram Marketing is so effective is that it removes the barriers of traditional advertising and introduces your brand to a new audience. This can be done via a more trustworthy source, most preferably, your influencer partner or a hired social media marketing expert.

The content of this eBook aims to enlighten you more about Instagram Marketing. Additionally, what the top influencers and brand know that you do not about the hottest social media will be expounded in depth.

What to Do When Getting Started on Instagram

You may have heard all the reasons why Instagram is a great marketing tool for business. Perhaps, you are using it for personal use. Even so, you may not have any idea about using Instagram for business purposes, especially for marketing your products or services. Below are simple steps of getting started on Instagram.

Download the Application

Instagram is primarily a mobile platform and can be downloaded and installed on any mobile device. Moreover, it can also be accessed via the web version. You can view the web version once you have set up your account. It is imperative to note that the majority of your activity will take place within the mobile app.

Choose a Noticeable Username

After signing up for Instagram with either an email address or a personal Facebook account, you will be prompted to choose a username. Ideally, it is prudent to select a recognizable username which can easily be associated with the organization's name. Remember that your username will be displayed publicly, and is what people see when they find you on Instagram. When setting up a business account, enter the full name of the business, which will make it easier for people to find you through the search function.

UPDATE YOUR PROFILE

Instagram allows you to fill out a bio about your business or yourself for a personal account. Due to text limitation, you are required to create a clear and precise description about who you are and what you offer. In case you are confined to a certain area, do not hesitate to add your location. It is also important to add the business website, which users can visit for more information.

UPLOAD A PROFILE PICTURE

It is crucial to add a photo that is recognizable to the people who know your business as well as potential customers. In most cases, the most viable and appropriate choice is your business logo. A logo is a perfect choice because most people can easily associate the logo with your business. You can only update your profile photo through a mobile device. Therefore, you can transfer your logo to your mobile device or use the import function, which enables you to draw pictures from Facebook and Twitter.

Alternatively, you can take a new photo with the application.

Post Your First Photo

Now that your profile is set up, you can go on and take your first photo. As mentioned above, you can take a new photo, import from Facebook or Twitter or upload from the files on your mobile device. If you are uploading a picture, you will have the chance to crop it to the desired size. Thereafter, you will have various options for different enhancements including filtering and adding borders. While uploading, you can tag people from your current location.

Tell Other Users You Are On Instagram

Use your existing social media channels to let people know that your business is now on Instagram. This is very important as people will continue living oblivious of your presence on Instagram. You need to tell your existing clients that they can view your communications via Instagram. If you have an email list with your customers, it will be okay to send a notification and request them to follow you for prompt communication.

Start Following Others

Search for your clients and start following them. For a personal account, you can ask your friends to give you their usernames so that you can follow them. In addition, you can search people and businesses using their hashtag, which they may give you beforehand. Following more people and businesses is a great way to make new connections and offer inspiration.

GET SOCIAL AND POST MORE PICTURES

Having learned the basics, set up your account, followed people and businesses, it is now time to start building a presence on Instagram. This can only be done by engaging with the people who are following you. Upload pictures on a regular basis and respond to tags by others. Avoid going for a long time without posting a new picture since your account will lose its attractiveness.

After following the steps above, you will be able to start using Instagram easily. Even so, you are required to carry out some research to ensure that you are posting the right pictures for your specific niche. Without a doubt, it will be self-damaging to post pictures that do not match your niche. This will only be deemed to be a high degree of losing focus as well as having no awareness of what you are really dealing with as a business. You can find a business in your niche and evaluate what they post and when they tend to post it. Even if you want to be unique and differentiate your business from the competition, it is essential to know what your competitors are doing. This will help you get the right pictures and also assist you in remaining focused on your niche.

SIMPLE INSTAGRAM TIPS FOR BEGINNERS

After getting started on Instagram, you need to know some simple dos and don'ts that will make you effective. Do not forget that you want to grow your business by using integral marketing and therefore understanding what exactly you are required to do will be of paramount importance. Below is a list of simple tips to help beginners to get the best out of Instagram as a platform for marketing.

USE HASHTAGS IN MODERATION

Using hashtags is an excellent way to increase your reach on Instagram, foster more engagement with existing followers, and even attract new followers. Tactlessly, some people take it too far by bloating their captions with hashtags which may not even be relevant to the topic of the photo. When you are using hashtags, ensure that you keep it at a minimum and only use keywords and captions that are relevant to your photo.

POST INTERSECTING PHOTOS AND VIDEOS

While using Instagram for marketing purposes, you should be keen on providing value for your followers. You can do this by evoking feelings with the photos and videos you post. Posts that arouse happiness, humor, motivation, nostalgia, love, or any other feeling will go a long way towards engaging your audience. Ensure that you post only high-quality photos with lots of colors because they tend to get the most action on Instagram.

DO NOT OVERDO THE PHOTOS WITH FILTERS

Notably, Instagram provides users with a bunch of filters that can be applied to photos to automatically enhance the look and style. Even though filter effects may be tempting, it is wise to limit their use and keep the color and contrast normal in most of your photos. However, avoid overdoing it. Actually, you can even avoid it completely if you have taken the photo with an HD camera. Always remember that people are amused by photos and videos which are colorful and natural looking.

MAKE POSTS OFTEN AND MAKE THEM INTERESTING

Keeping your followers interested and engaged requires you to create new content on a regular basis. That does not mean that you should post 10 photos within a day. Preferably, being frequent and posting new content at least once every other day would be better. Moreover, make the content more interesting. Avoid going for long periods of time without posting, lest you start losing followers.

INTERACT WITH YOUR FOLLOWERS

Make time to interact with your followers as well as to comment on various replies. Never ignore the followers who regularly like and comment on your posts. Instead, take it that you have a following and make them valued. The best practice is to reply to their comments. In addition, you can go ahead and view their account and like a few of their photos.

DO NOT PURCHASE FOLLOWERS

Nowadays, you can buy Instagram followers, just the way you can boost a post on Facebook. Even though it is true that you can obtain a huge number of followers cheaply, it is not the best way to go. The problem with buying Instagram followers is that they are fake and inactive. This means that they are not real people and you are not able to engage with them. It looks awkward and bizarre to see an account with 15K followers but no comments or likes on your photos and videos. Instead, formulate a plan to get followers naturally.

MIND THE LATEST INSTAGRAM TRENDS

Be on the lookout of new things the moment they are introduced. Evidently, hashtags and shout-outs are great, but will these two will eventually become outdated. This makes it important to pay attention to the latest trends, especially when you are using Instagram for marketing. Avoid getting left behind and putting yourself at risk of losing valuable followers because you are unaware of the latest trends.

CONTACT SPECIFIC USERS VIA INSTAGRAM DIRECT

Even as you focus on frequent updates on Instagram, ensure that you contact some of your followers directly. We cannot refute that public posts get to most of your followers but it is important to target some of your followers by privately direct messaging them with the intended photo or video. Instagram direct is the best way to get in touch with a specific group of users without the need to broadcast the content to everyone.

FIND NEW CONTENT USING THE EXPLORE TAB

Basically, the explore tab on Instagram is a segment where the most popular photos and videos get featured. Photos included in this segment are customized according to the photos and videos that have been liked and commented by people you follow. In fact, you can scoop the chance and find new users to follow or engage with by checking out the tab on a regular basis.

With the tips above, you will surely make the best out of marketing. There is nothing as perfect as knowing what is required of you, especially when it comes to using Instagram for personal or marketing purposes.

CHAPTER 2: BUILDING A STRONG INSTAGRAM PROFILE

HOW TO CREATE A PERFECT INSTAGRAM NAME

Choosing the perfect Instagram is crucial. Your name should be simple and, most preferably, similar to the website domain name of your business website. People need to get you simply and directly. This implies that your name should be recognizable and pop up right away during a search. When thinking about the username to apply, craft it in a way that will inspire a good idea about your niche to your followers. Remember that you are not a world-famous brand or celebrity who can easily get a following within a few minutes of launching a new channel.

It certainly makes sense to come up with the best Instagram name after learning about individuals or businesses who fail to grow on Instagram before they even start. Mainly, this can be caused by people getting disappointed or confused when they see content that does not match your name.

In short, do not rush into picking an Instagram name. Instead, take time, consult, and research the best names in your niche before settling on a name. You can ask friends, family or anybody else you trust how your choice of name sounds and whether it is best suited to be a perfect Instagram name. In fact, you can use another technique to know whether you have a perfect name. Just tell them your Instagram name and notice their first reaction after hearing it. This way, you will get natural honest feedback about your choice of name.

Even as you can do all this, below are a couple of things to watch out for when creating your Instagram name.

MAKE IT EASY TO PRONOUNCE

A good Instagram name should be easy to pronounce. People should find it easy to repeat the name without necessarily having to write it down. Preferably, make it similar to your brand name, which may be known to some people. No part of your name should be confusing.

LET IT BE UNIQUE

It is obvious that you cannot use a username that has already been taken by another user. You need to create your unique name to avoid similarities to any other business or brands. In any case, copying a username or applying a slight change may come back to bite you with copyright infringement problems, especially when your page begins to grow.

USE PERIODS AND UNDERSCORES

Creating a unique name for your account may necessitate the use of periods and underscores. At first, you may want to avoid them completely but it might not be realistic. Nevertheless, avoid using two or more periods or underscores right beside one another. This is because it makes it harder for people to find you easily. For example, the search engines will treat King_Klugger.Kugger as three different words, making the discovery of your account more difficult.

DO NOT MAKE IT TOO LONG

A good Instagram name should not be lengthy, either for a personal or business account. Using such a name will negate the important point stated above; make it easy to pronounce! Look at what the other famous pages have as their name and learn. Conciseness and clarity are key to a perfect Instagram name because shorter names are easier to search and provide exclusivity.

AVOID GENDER, ETHNIC OR RELIGION BIASED NAMES

When using Instagram for marketing purposes, do not rule out the fact that you are dealing with people of different gender, race, ethnicity, religion, amongst others. In reference to this, your name should not reflect any of these contentious factors if you want to be successful in Instagram. On the other hand, you can post biased content depending on your niche. For instance, if you deal with women's beauty products, it will not become an issue when you only post feminine-based content. In short, you have to respect the diversity of your followers in terms of all these natural factors.

AVOID COMMON NAMES

When making your Instagram name, avoid common words such as success, billionaire, business etc. just go for a unique name that does not include these common names. Bear in mind that you will be up against Instagram accounts that dominate your niche. You will be facing a steep uphill climb when you do not stand out as unique.

Having learned the tips for creating a perfect Instagram name, do not hesitate to make yourself the best name you can get. It will count when it comes to gaining more followers, visibility, and overall enhancement in Instagram marketing efforts.

THE HIGH IMPACT IMAGE - THE LOGO

You may have written and executed a social media marketing campaign for your business, except for one thing. You do not have a logo design. A logo is your branding and it is absolutely critical in any marketing strategy. If you have a logo, people will forever associate your business with that logo every moment they see it. This implies that a logo is an important part of branding, especially if you are really want to make the best out of social media and appropriately market your business online.

Most notably, a logo gives brand recognition to potential and existing customers. Also, it gives brand recognition to your target audience. When anyone within your target audience sees your logo online, they will be obligated to learn more about what you do professionally and what you offer as a business.

So, exactly where does your logo fit into social media marketing? Even though a logo is small in size, it is an extremely important component that contributes to the success of any social media campaign. As a marketer or influencer, it is imperative to make existing and potential customers see your logo on a daily basis. You can embed it in your photos, maybe in one corner. Alternatively, you can add it as a watermark on publications posted on any of your social media platforms. This way, your customers will form a perception of your company that will stay with them forever. The logo plays a very important part in your social media marketing campaign in several ways, as described below.

PROMOTING YOUR BUSINESS

People may not know how a logo may sell a business to the public. Well, it is an important image that has a tendency of sticking in the minds of most people. Typically, your logo design speaks for itself when it comes to promoting your business. You do not need to say a word after showing someone the logo of your business. A good logo will say so much about what you stand for and what you are offering, without necessarily uttering any words. For instance, you do not have to be told what that tick-like logo on your pair of shoes, cap, or training gear means! The logo tells you all about the manufacturer, right?

PROVIDES AN IDENTITY

Content may not be enough to get the word out there. You will only fail if you post content without any real sense of identity with regard to your branding in the form of a logo. In fact, you will end up like all of the other start-up marketers on the internet who create and post a high volume of content in the hopes of generating a lot of traffic to your website. This approach of posting a series of posts may produce some results. Nevertheless, your logo will greatly communicate who you are and what your business is all about. In many instances, the logo will attract people so much that they are fascinated enough to want to know more about your products and services.

DEMONSTRATES PROFESSIONALISM

Including a logo on every Instagram marketing post will show a high sense of professionalism. Your customers will feel comfortable while doing business with you. Additionally, if you have an interesting, attractive and good-quality logo design, it will be outstanding on whatever you are sharing with your audience. In time, you will notice that the logo may be enough to get the audience to want to build a relationship with you. If they like your logo, they will like your creativity and the way in which you communicate. Most importantly, they will love what you are selling and buy.

A LOGO ILLUMINATES WHO AND WHAT YOU ARE

When starting to post and share content, it is of the essence to place your logo on your content with a link back to your website. In turn, your followers will start visiting your website often. This is where you will begin to reap the benefits of the content that you are sharing and syndicating. Therefore, start to believe in your credibility. Know that when people trust your credibility and expertise, they will want to be involved with you and your business. In Instagram marketing, this is your ultimate objective.

Even as a logo gives all the stated benefits, there are several things that you need to consider before coming up with the final logo for any marketing campaign.

- You should carry out extensive research before creating your logo. Typically, the logo must be perfectly synonymous with your brand and theme colors. You should make the logo and brand one and the same thing.

- Select an effective logo name, which is unique and memorable. If your logo involves abbreviations/letters, ensure that it easily falls off everyone's tongue. Simply make it easy to pronounce and uncomplicated.

- You want your logo to be pleasing to the eye of everyone in the audience. Altogether, make it simple and easy to identify with.

- In case you are not sure whether or not your logo will be effective and powerful, a good way to gather information is through focus groups. The easiest way to do this is to form a group and invite people whose opinions and judgment you value. Take time to evaluate their feedback and implement the most viable options.

WHAT TO CONSIDER WHEN CREATING THE PERFECT LOGO

There are a number of aspects that go into a logo design including, fonts, tagline, colors, and more. When designing what may seem to be a social media-approved logo, you need to keep in mind the variables. Also, keep in mind that even if you end up with a perfect logo, it may not necessarily work out on every social media platform. These tips will help you create a logo that will give you an attractive online presence.

- Be mindful of your aspect ratio. Some social media sites will require you to convert your logo to a square or reduce the measurements to nearly square-shaped thumbnail. Even so, your logo does not have to be perfectly square but should have the flexibility of being easily converted to one. When posting your logo, it is unnecessary to make use of all the space you have to avoid compressing or reducing it to fit into the small space.

- Be consistent on all social media platforms. With an effective social media strategy, your logo will be seen on a variety of sites including your website, Twitter, Facebook, YouTube channel, to name a few. Due to this, it is wise to have one logo you use for every site. Consistency will impact an unending image of your logo to your audience and they will easily recognize and link it to your business.

- Use detached text and graphics when designing. Ensure your text and graphics are separate components of your logo. This will help if it ever requires converting your logo to a different size. Actually, some companies use a single graphic or a single letter in social media for ease of conversion and overall use.

- If you have an intricate logo, you should know that simplicity matters. Further, you may be facing the risk of some of the logo elements not being recognizable when resized. For this reason, avoid long taglines, thin lines, and detailed graphics when designing your logo. Altogether, limit colors and shades. The truth is that a logo which is created with two to three colors will work better on social media because it stands out and is visible from afar. If you do not have any idea how to make a logo in line with these guidelines, engage an expert logo maker.

In a nutshell, your logo is extremely important when it comes to the overall success of your social media marketing campaign. It identifies you, the business, and what you are selling. This compels people to want to become loyal customers to your brand. Surely, there are many components that make up a successful social media marketing campaign, and even though the logo is physically a small part of it, it has a huge impact.

CONTENTS OF A GREAT INSTAGRAM BIO

It is prudent to comprehend the components that make up an Instagram bio. Once this is done, you can add more details and polish your accounts to ensure that users understand exactly what you are about and what they should expect when they follow you. The problems that you may have while doing your bio is the little space you have. The Instagram section where you are supposed to make your bio only allows 150 characters. Additionally, your username must fit under 30 characters. With over 800 million users on the app, you need to put all your chances of getting discovered and followed for effective marketing and influencing activities. So, what exactly are the components of an Instagram bio in a business account? Below are key bio components which may have a negative impact on Instagram marketing if not created the right way.

A PROFILE PHOTO

The profile page should ideally comprise of a profile photo that is relevant to your business or brand. The photo may be a logo or a product photo. Whatever you select to be your profile photo, it should be attractive and easily associated with your business. Most notably, some companies, celebrities, and influencers find it wise to use a verified badge on their profile photo to identify themselves.

It is important to note that Instagram crops the uploaded profile photo into a circle. This implies that your profile photo will remain visible and with the right clarity even after cropping. You should not worry about uploading a photo with a square shape featuring your brand photo or logo right at the center. After all, the corners will be cut off without cutting off your branding.

USERNAME AND NAME

The username appears at the top of the profile page while your name will be in a more prominent spot and bolded on the profile. Both the username and name are searchable in the Instagram search field. Therefore, as mentioned earlier, carefully select both your username and name. If you have a simple and short business name, search results should show your profile straight away. After the search, the name will appear in gray under the profile's handle.

PUBLIC PROFILE

As a marketer or influencer, you will be shooting yourself in the foot if your profile is not public. In the event that your profile is private, anyone visiting your profile will not be able to view your photos. This will deter them from following you. To avoid all this, ensure that your profile is public by going to settings and toggling the "Private Account" setting to turn it off. Typically, if you have an Instagram business profile, it is automatically public.

BIO

Here, you need to create a short description and sum up about you or your business. Most companies use this space to give a list of products or services they offer, their location, website, and physical address. Make it short and direct to the point since you can only type 150 characters.

WEBSITE

In the bio, you can include your website to make your business more visible, as well as encourage more people to visit the business website for more information. In this field, ensure you add a link to your website.

CATEGORY

This feature is only available for a business account. The category that appears under a company's name is directly linked to the one that is selected on the related Facebook page. For example, indicating that you are in the restaurant business or a public figure is as easy as choosing the appropriate category.

CALL-TO-ACTION BUTTONS

Ensure you activate the call-to-action buttons by filling in the necessary information that includes an email address, phone number, and location. Previously, business account users were writing their email addresses and location address in the bio section. This feature has been added for business account set up to free up some space in the bio section. Nevertheless, this feature is only shown in the app view and not the web view. This field under the call-to-action function can be found by clicking Edit profile and then Contact Options.

EMAIL

Adding an email address to the bio generates an email button on the profile. When one clicks on the email, they will be prompted to open the default mail app on their devices. This will make it easy for your followers and potential customers to communicate with you via email.

DIRECTIONS

If you want to give your location, this is the field you should enter your physical address and help customers find you easily. When clients click on this button, it will prompt them to a map application on their device.

CALL

The best and most convenient contact information is adding your business phone number. After all, using a phone call makes communication more personal.

When someone clicks on the call button, they will be prompted to use the default call application.

Recently, Instagram released a new feature that allows you to include hashtags and profile links in a bio. This creates a wide range of possibilities for marketers to use hashtags. For example, if your brand has a number of Instagram handles for various parts of your business, you can include a link to your other handles in your bio instead of making your followers search for them. This makes it easier for people to find your handles, especially when your accounts are not yet verified.

Once you understand how to utilize and complete the components of your bio, you will effectively increase visibility and relevancy. Your account will make more sense to all your followers. After all, your main purpose on Instagram is to be clear to them.

HOW TO WRITE AN INSTAGRAM BIO THAT WILL MAKE AN IMPRESSION

As seen above, an Instagram bio tells the followers and other users about the nature of your business. Basically, it is a short description of yourself. To make an impression, the bio must be precise and catchy. Let it lure people into following you as well as want to do business with you. If Instagram marketing and influencing is your main objective, ensure that you come up with a killer bio. Below are several tips that will help you to create a flawless bio.

INCLUDE A TAGLINE

You can use an exceptional tagline in your bio to make your bio provocative and fascinating. A tagline will enable you to tell individuals precisely what your company does in very few words. Likewise, you can also use a summary of the company's values or add the mission statement in the bio.

BE MINIMALISTIC

A perfect Instagram bio must be short and as simple as possible. Simply give as much information as a targeted customer would require to recognize the basic aim of your brand. Obviously, your visitors can browse through your Instagram posts or visit your website to find out more about your business.

LINK YOUR INSTAGRAM WITH OTHER SOCIAL MEDIA ACCOUNTS

This will enable you to be more efficient in keeping the account bio short and to the point. Linking the account with your accounts on Facebook, Twitter, and Snapchat will allow your followers to easily find your company on other social media platforms. This implies that you will have more visibility and higher chances of getting a wide clientele.

USE A BRANDED HASHTAG

An account that utilizes user-generated content for making their Instagram account can incorporate an appropriate branded hashtag in their bio. Nothing creates a more convincing brand story than images of real people interacting with your brand. The most effortless approach to collect those images is to include a branded hashtag in your bio that gives Instagram users a simple way to share their content for you on your own feed.

Note that branded hashtags are not just for products. For instance, some service providers combine an emoji and a branded hashtag to set up a feed that humanizes their brands and make it look more engaging. Bear in mind that the hashtags you use are only clickable in the Instagram web interface and not in the mobile application.

EMBRACE EMOJIS

Using emojis can really go a long way towards helping a user to convey the personality and identity of a business. Otherwise, emojis can be used as a replacement for certain words. Emojis also make Instagram posts and bios appear more exciting.

Even though using emojis might feel excessively cutesy, you may want to consider incorporating them in the Instagram bio toolbox. From faces to animals to other restrained symbols, whichever emoji you choose will create a sense of brand personality. Remarkably, an emoji can be worth a thousand words and can tell more about your product or services in a few words. Some people actually find it easy to use an emoji to communicate briefly what could have taken several minutes to compose in words.

USE LINE BREAKS TO YOUR INSTAGRAM BIO

Using line breaks in an Instagram bio serves as a clear illustration of your expertise in Instagram and its features. Even more, it makes a profile look more engaging and consumable. Line breaks enable you to break the bio into information that is easy for visitors to read through. Therefore, you can easily highlight the most important things about the business you are carrying out on Instagram.

INCLUDE AN APPEALING CALL TO ACTION

When creating a perfect bio, bear in mind that you cannot avoid a proper call to action. Actually, without it the bio is incomplete. The call to action should drive your targeted audience to visit your store, call or email you for more information. Including a call to action is important in any Instagram marketing post. Ask yourself what exactly you want visitors to do after viewing your profile.

For instance, you may want people to like your Facebook page, sign up for your newsletter, order your products directly from your site, or take any action that aligns to your marketing goals. Additionally, be clear in asking your visitors and potential customers to take any steps. Do not tell them to do something that will deter them from following you or doing business with you. For example, if your aim is to build an Instagram following, the most appropriate call to action would simply be to ask your visitor to follow your feed.

INCLUDE YOUR CONTACT INFORMATION

Providing a contact in your bio is essential. Just imagine having a follower who is really impressed by your business and wants to get in touch with you but does not have the contact. This necessitates the need to include your contact information in your bio. It may be a phone number or an email address. Rather than just leaving a comment in posts, users can reach you directly.

STATE WHAT MAKES YOU SPECIAL

What makes you unique compared to your competitors? State it in your bio and you will see the impact. Notably, customers want to get the best there is in the market and preferably from the most unique seller. When marketing, clearly indicate what makes you outstanding.

A good Instagram profile should accurately describe what the business is about and what it can perfectly deliver. Unique skills and services should be provided to lure potential clients into not only following you but to buying and making consecutive purchases from your business. Include other fun facts that you can about your brand, because it is a great way to showcase the company's personality.

HIGHLIGHT YOUR HOURS OF OPERATION

People want to know the time they can visit your business. While it may be to search it on your website, add this information to your Instagram profile. It makes your followers aware of the hours of operation and will visit you in good time. You can also include a location application that may help them find your physical location much easier.

With these ideas to make a perfect Instagram bio, you are ready to create a bio that will impeccably showcase your intention on Instagram. Also, you will effectively drive your visitors to like, follow, and even buy with a just 150 characters persuasion.

Chapter 3: How to Grow Big in Instagram

Finding Your Instagram Niche

Undoubtedly, Instagram is growing and it is has become the favorite for most social media marketers and influencers. As a business owner, marketer or influencer, having a niche-oriented Instagram account is essential to connect with the right audience. Finding a niche will prove to be helpful in obtaining a huge following as well as making an impact on your sale and marketing strategy.

At first, some people get into Instagram to socialize and for fun. Anyway, it is a better way to share some of your personal photos and perhaps show off! In addition, Instagram can be used for an effective and fruitful marketing strategy. Most of the people on Instagram are unaware that you can make their business more visible. However, this becomes better when you have clearly identified your niche. Most of the prevalent niches are fashion, health, and fitness, travel and tourism and beauty. It should not be an issue if your business does not fall under any of these niches. Start by evaluating the most appropriate niche for your business which makes you unique.

There is an Instagram niche for everyone, whether you are a succulent grower, food blogger, nature lover, or a travel marketer. You just need to find your niche and stick to it. Doing this may not be easy; take time deliberating the best choice. It also requires accuracy and patience. Here is how to find your Instagram niche.

DISCOVER WHAT YOU ARE GOOD AT AND WHAT YOU LIKE

The first step in finding an Instagram niche is asking yourself what interests you. Most preferably, it should be something that you have a love for. Maybe you have an undying interest in beauty. This implies that you can go for a beauty niche on Instagram. It is prudent to have a niche that you are passionate about. It can be very costly to venture and invest in a niche that you may not have a liking for to avoid getting bored and leaving it along the way.

Before selecting an Instagram niche, take time to do a soul search. Eventually, you will land on the best niche. In case it sounds cliché, doing it with passion will make others take note, become interested, and start liking your unique niche. If you are at crossroads regarding the right niche, you can ask for an honest opinion from a close friend, a relative or colleague. They will definitely tell you what you are capable of perfecting.

At first, you can use different styles of photography such as minimal, saturated, black and white, landscape or portrait, and moody, amongst others. This will help you to take note of the style of photography your audience likes the most. Once you are past the initial stage of finding what your followers like, stick to it, because chances are you may lose some followers who are only interested in your style.

FIND A UNIQUE COLOR SCHEME

When it comes to an Instagram niche, first impression always counts. People only need half a second to decide whether or not to follow you. Therefore, make an impression by continually having the right color collection and array. Some people are passive users, especially during busy hours of the day. If you want to lure them into following you, you will need to impress them the first time they land on your profile. Most likely, people will look at your profile through the little grid format before they decide to follow you.

You can take a small survey to study the most liked colors. This can be done in a silent manner which only involves creating a color scheme and later noticing the feedback on different color schemes. This way you will get to know the color that excites most of your followers.

BE CONSISTENT

Being consistent is a reliable approach to add credibility to your niche. In fact, adding credibility to your brand through Instagram is similar to blogging. It requires consistency in posting new content, being creative, and maybe letting your followers know when they can expect the next update from you. If you intend to build your niche through frequent postings, you can make use of the Instagram feature.

Even with this feature at your exposure, avoid posting more than once in every 6 hours. Additionally, do not post more than three times a day. If you have taken time to study most Instagram users, they detest being spammed. Do not lose followers for making seemingly numerous content.

Regardless of what niche you choose, branding your Instagram account is a great way to market your products and services. You can also drive more traffic on your website and make more sales, which translates to more income.

SPYING ON BIGGER AUTHORITY PAGES ON YOUR NICHE

It is true that every business faces competition. In fact, if you have no competition, there is definitely a big problem! Simply, it means that no investor believes in the possibility of making money in your industry. Therefore, having competitors should make you happy and find a reason to put more effort into your business. This competition trickles down to your marketing strategies, maintaining sales volumes among every business activities. Overall, competition is a major problem which can lead to your downfall because it takes away customers. Acquiring new customers may be difficult.

Nowadays, a company without a strong social media campaign and an on-going engagement plan with customers leaves money on the table. Having stated that competition affects all aspects of a business, it also affects your Instagram marketing strategy. Growing your number of followers on Instagram requires you to measure up to your competitors. Even without copying, you must be ready to do exactly or close to what they are doing to obtain and sustain new followers. This is done by spying on what they are doing to achieve a huge following.

Moreover, you should spy on what bigger authority pages are doing to help you perfect your Instagram marketing strategy. Below are approaches which you can use to spy authority sites with a huge following.

USE SPECIAL TOOLS FOR SPYING

Observing the moves of your competitors can help you compete and find loopholes in your social media marketing strategy. Getting to know what competitors and big businesses are doing to get ahead is part of the entrepreneurial game. Presently, there are many ways to spy on your competitors as well as bigger authority sites. However, you should know the easiest of them all to avoid wasting time doing manual work. There is software and tools you can work with to get all the information on the moves of authority pages on Instagram. You can simply automate this activity while you concentrate on creating your own strategy. Use tools like Sprout Social, Phlanx, and Social Blade, amongst others

TRACK COMPETING AND BIG BRANDS

You should get more advanced than just spying on competition and start monitoring brands. Following companies such as NFL, Starbucks, amongst others with big pages on Instagram will enable you to notice what they are doing. In addition, you will also see what people are saying about them. In turn, this can help you improve your marketing strategy and become aligned with important and profitable activities.

In this era, people are sharing every piece of information including the experience they had buying or being served from a business premises. Such is the information that you should be looking for Instagram. Make use of both positive and negative feedback. Of course, the negative will help you capitalize on the weaknesses of your competitors while the positive will act as a basis to benchmark the quality of your products or services. In simple words, use Instagram as the network and you will continually see the Instagram mentions and the feedback that users transmit throughout social media related to your business, competitors, and leading brands in your industry.

FOLLOW YOUR COMPETITORS AND BIG COMPANIES

You can spy your competitors by following them on Instagram, and maybe on all social media platforms, to see how they engage with their followers. However, try not to follow them using your brand profile. They will definitely know that you are spying on them. Use a pseudo account or just create one with a real name and use them to follow competitors and authority pages.

Why is it important to track the activities of your competitors and big authority pages? Mainly, you will benefit from tips and simple tricks they employ, but they do not give them explicitly. Moreover, you will learn how they reply to comments, what they like and share. The main objective here is to assess how promptly they give feedback to issues raised by their followers. Obviously, bigger authority pages like Red Bull, Adidas Original and others have timely and helpful feedback which may help you improve how you deal with your followers.

SEARCH THEIR BRANDED HASHTAGS

According to social media experts, one must have a specific hashtag to represent your brand on Instagram. Obviously, your competitors and authority pages use branded hashtags.

Besides help from spying tools, invest some time in research of your own. Follow posts from competitors and authority pages. Ultimately, you will learn and appreciate the various ways in which they use hashtags. You will notice that they use branded hashtags. Afterward, search for the hashtags on Instagram to see who else is using them and interact with them. There is a high tendency that you will lure some to buying from you.

In order to smooth the progress of your job, you need to find the hashtag used by authority pages, which is like a tagline for the business and search for it on the platform. Get more information and know how they present themselves to their audience and how their audience sees them.

Chapter 4: Instagram Content

How to Create Excellent Quality Engaging Images and Content

The key to achieving the desired following on Instagram is creating catchy and engaging images and content. Nevertheless, the issue remains how one can create excellent quality images and content. The process may take time, needs persistence, and commitment. Below are tips to help you create brilliant image and content.

Research and Understand Your Audience

Once you have a content creation strategy, you need to be mindful of the audience who will see, hear, and watch the content. Never forget that effective content is not about topics you personally want to talk about. Actually, your content should be made out in the open with the involvement, feedback, and direction of your audience.

A tremendous content marketing strategy should be designed to answer the most pressing issues emanating from the audience. Aim to educate and transform your audience. The only way that the content will connect with the audience is making it in a way that will speak directly to them. You must have empathy and understanding of what they are currently going through. To know more about your audience, engage them more, notice their preferences, and implement your content strategy based on this.

DIVERSIFY YOUR CONTENT

The easiest way to create engaging content is to avoid sticking to one type of medium to communicate with your followers. Changing the content per post is a way of diversifying. This implies that if you are used to writing text-based blogs, it is high time to start varying it with things such as graphics, images, quotes, videos, and more. Think of making your content with different styles including humor. It is healthy to add some "spice" to your content once in a while.

TAKE BETTER PICTURES

The main idea behind incorporating images in your profile is building trust and legitimacy about your product. Evidently, this cannot be done when you use irrelevant images. If you want to use pictures from a camera, as opposed to the downloaded ones, it is highly recommendable to have a high-quality camera. On the other hand, you can use your Smartphone to take good pictures. Even though most people think they share captivating images on Instagram, they miss out on one very important principle. You do not just need to share good quality pictures. They should match your brand.

EDIT THE IMAGES

Once you have chosen the most outstanding photo, edit it for a better effect. Even without a computer-based photo editor, you can use any of the readily available free mobile applications to improve the quality of photo. While on a computer, the obvious software is Photoshop. However, the software is not intuitive and requires some learning and practice before getting to know how to effectively use it. With photo editing software, any shot can be transformed into a well-defined infographic. Notably, infographics are the trending and most excellent method of images in your social media content.

FOCUS ON THE CONTRAST AND BALANCE

An image must have the right contrast to stand out in an Instagram feed. The contrast may include colors, shapes, fonts, light, exposure, scale, and spaces. You should find the right scale which makes the image stand out. It is a crucial step in getting your followers to engage with content you post.

INSERT QUOTES ON PHOTOS

Presently, photos with embedded quotes are on the rise and very popular in terms of engagement and response generation. You can copy and paste a famous and inspiring quote and place it in the appropriate image. Good quotes are readily available and can be found online. It is easy to understand why pictures containing quotes are effective. They are inspirational and reading them may make your audience feel good.

LEAVE WHITE SPACE AND BORDERS ON IMAGES

Leaving white edges around your Instagram images can create an extraordinary effect which attracts the eye more than an image with no border. This is especially true if the image is of the right size and has excellent clarity. Borders help to ensure that elements in your design have room to be conspicuous. This is an important aspect to consider if you want to avoid an overly busy post.

THE IMPORTANCE OF BEING TRANSPARENT ON SOCIAL MEDIA

Transparency amounts to building trust and is an extremely important component for sustaining any relationship. Further, trust is built through honesty and keeping promises. It is imperative to note that you value transparency even while dealing with a social media audience, without whom you will not have anyone to address in your page. Notably, being transparent while dealing with your Instagram audience is taken for granted, oblivious of the impact it may have on the overall effectiveness of any marketing campaign. Transparency is a surefire way of building a huge following on Instagram and increasing the company's marketing strategy and profitability. Here are some reasons why you should be transparent on Instagram.

INCREASES CUSTOMER LOYALTY

Most of your followers may be your customers who require the best customer support. In customer relations, transparency goes a long way towards fostering trust and customer loyalty. This may take time, but with consistency and diligent efforts, you will eventually win the hearts existing and potential customers with transparency. It costs nothing to be transparent. All you are required to do is be honest in your communication and in addressing customers issues. In short, make Instagram posts with honesty and utmost good faith

BOOSTS THE BUSINESS REPUTATION

The brand and reputation of the company rise with increased transparency. Satisfied customers will definitely let others know about the great experiences they have while dealing with your company. In this way, satisfied customers will make recommendations about your business even without your knowledge. When such comments and discussions become common, especially on Instagram and other social media platforms, your business obtains an excellent reputation. Sooner than later, your business will become well known for transparency and good practices.

PROMPTS FEEDBACK FROM YOUR AUDIENCE

With transparency, the relationship between your business and your followers will lead to an open communication. Customers will be more willing to offer their suggestions and feedback and help your business to make improvements in areas of weakness. Moreover, you will get an honest view of our products or services, even if the feedback is based on criticism. Certainly, you can obtain new ideas from the feedback given by your Instagram followers. This will simply make innovation and creativity easier for your company. Taking into account and making products that conform to the expectations and preferences of customers will further enhance the reputation of such companies.

IMPROVE CUSTOMER SERVICE

Transparency is essential in good customer relations practice. Considering the feedback given by social media followers and addressing them promptly can prove helpful in enhancing customer service. It makes them feel like they are being heard and valued. Therefore, take time to collect, scrutinize, and act on the feedback given online. After all, your followers are only acting on the basis of transparency and freely speaking their mind.

BOOSTS FOLLOWER'S TRUST IN YOUR BUSINESS

This benefit of being transparent is almost not worth mentioning given its obviousness. Consumers trust companies that are open and truthful with them, even on social media. With the rise of communication via social media, including Instagram, it is important to manage the business image. With transparency and high levels of trust from customers and social media followers, companies are able to manage issues much better, as they are given a chance to redeem themselves. In the event of a challenge, customers and social media followers will not be quick to jump to conclusions and opinions until such time that the company is able to respond. This is a major advantage of transparency and trust building that sustains the image and reputation of a company.

Transparency in social media and overall customer relations is not just a trend in the business world that has suddenly kicked off and will die with time. It is an approach that social media marketers, influencers and companies must embrace to promote deeper.

USE STORIES TO GET MORE PERSONAL WITH YOUR FOLLOWERS

Some people get confused when it comes to Instagram stories and posts. However, there is a huge difference between the two. Instagram stories are not posts. Instagram posts appear in a user's feed and will permanently remain on the profile page unless deleted. Users can save posts and revisit them at any time in the future.

On the other hand, Instagram stories are found above the home feed. They are easily accessible by clicking on the small circles showing a user's profile picture. Typically, you can start at the beginning of the story feed by clicking on the first bubble or just settling on watching a specific one. Whichever way you decide, the stories will automatically continue playing until you have watched them all. Stories disappear after 24 hours.

You can use stories to become more personal with your followers. You can achieve this by posting stories that directly arouse feelings in your followers. Stories that some followers have ever experienced or are presently experiencing can be of greater impact. Further, you can tell stories with a moral lesson. This way, your stories will be more personal to your followers and they will want to read more and more.

So, why do you need to use Instagram stories?

Marketers and influencers demonstrate diversity and creativity by creating various content on social media platforms. Instagram stories are an integral part of remaining relevant to your Instagram followers. The following major justifications are reasons why you should use Instagram stories.

- Stories have high engagement rates. According to verified statistics, nearly 150 million users actively use Instagram stories every month. Instagram Stories also have a 28% higher average open rate than stories on other social media platforms. Most importantly, at least 25 people out of 100 who see the story will want to read through it. As a result, users are officially engaged and interested.

- With Instagram stories, you will have the full attention of your followers because they occupy a full mobile screen. A post will just occupy a small portion of the screen and may go unnoticed by followers.

- Stories flow continuously. Even if users may skip brand content in the feed, your content will absolutely pop up in their Stories stream. They can click past it if they want. However, since it is taking up the full screen, they will at least get a quick glance before clicking away.

With high willingness from users to engage, there is no doubt that businesses should be using a format that demands user attention. Using Instagram Stories in and of itself automatically increases the reach of your posts because users are extremely engaged with them.

HOW TO USE STORIES TO WIDEN YOU FAN BASE

Instagram stories are a great way to increase your following. Even so, some people do not know how to use this feature to get the desired following on Instagram. The good news is that using this feature has been made easy in this book and details about how to do so has also been shared. There are several tactics that can be used to grow your following with Instagram stories.

Generate Curiosity

The best way to use Instagram stories is creating curiosity. Just cut the story short at its peak, just when the reader wants to know what happened afterward. Tell the reader to read your next post. This way, you have all the attention of your audience and they will be keen to follow you for the next part of your story. Remember, failure to post the next part of your story will only amount to inconsistency, which will only make you lose your following.

STICK TO A THEME WITHIN YOUR NICHE

Social media experts have continually suggested that you should have a theme on your Instagram page. Likewise, your Instagram story should have a theme as well. Notably, the most important part of your story is sticking to your niche. For instance, you cannot be in a fashion niche and explain your trip to a fancy restaurant. This will be a total disconnect and your audience will notice a total disconnect. One thing is certain: sticking to a theme will enable you to attract people who share your love for that particular theme. This is how you will grow your following and fan base.

Ensure a Story Has Faces in It

People like seeing images in stories. Otherwise, they tend to become bored as soon as they start reading content with no images. According to a study conducted to establish the impact of images in encouraging readers, a one-page content with only one image can increase the motivation to read by 35 percent. This is no different when it comes to Instagram stories. Therefore, no matter how many stories you want to post on your page, make sure you embed at least one relevant image.

Use Color and Contrast to Your Advantage

Perfect Instagram posts are brighter and richer in blues, grays, and greens. This is as opposed to supersaturated posts that are dimmer and full of yellows, pinks, and oranges. However, it is good to know the color preference of your followers. Therefore, keep your story luminous and vibrant and all eyes will be on you. Actually, you can even include a color palette to be part of your theme.

AVOID THE FILTERS

Filters are known to be perfect when it comes to making photos look exceptional. The modest practice is to use photos in their original form. However, this requires the use of a high deification camera. According to most experienced social media specialists, Instagram content with no filters performs the best. If you have a High Definition camera, the better your image will be. You will not have to use the filters feature. Thus, even if you have a picture from the last 24 hours that was already filtered, stick with the original. Indeed, stories can be built using what you may consider "outtakes" form your day. Notably, an entire story can make for a delightful-behind-the scenes unfiltered look at your life.

BE COMMITTED AND POST REGULARLY

As a good practice for social media, you should post regularly. This can be linked to the tactic of generating curiosity. Once you create curiosity in your followers, remain committed to posting your stories. You should avoid going missing in action. If you do, your last post will become buried in everyone's feed and people will slowly start forgetting about you. The consensus seems to be that you should create one story every day. Since stories are ephemeral, try posting one regular photo to your profile grid, combined with one story per day.

Always remember that quality is superior to quantity. Posting 10 irrelevant posts per day will only make your followers flee. If you have nothing sensible to post, just kill your desire to put it on your Instagram. It is better to go for a whole day without sharing a story than post something that will somehow irritate your followers.

Chapter 5: Growing Your Fan Base

How to Time Your Instagram Posts and Shoutouts to Get More Engagement and Followers

Once you have created your Instagram page and communicated with followers on Instagram, the obvious next thing is to strategize on how to reach out a wider audience. Essentially, you need to know how to get a huge fan base without being someone famous beyond the Instagram community.

More so, you will want to know exactly how to get more free Instagram followers. One of the surest ways is through shoutouts. If you are willing to master this great follower-building trend, your page will become very popular in as little as a few weeks or months.

Basically, shoutouts are a form of advertising other pages, mainly done by authority pages and influencers. In a general sense, a shoutout is when a famous Instagrammer mentions you on their own account and then tells their fans or followers to

197

check you out and follow you too. Shoutouts are a great way of getting your name in front of a large number of users and potential followers. Unfortunately, getting a shoutout from the ever busy (and expensive) influencers and famous Instagrammers is not as easy as it sounds. It requires networking and being in continuous engagement with influencers. Sometimes, it also involves being willing to feature another users' content on your own feed as part of the shoutout agreement.

Timing is essential when it comes to shoutouts. On Instagram, you need a mention when there is a large audience for a shoutout to be effective. Even as you cannot dictate terms to whoever you want to mention you, request them to create the shoutout at a specific time. This requires you to carry out research and understand when most people are online and will see the shoutout. If the most suitable time (when most people use Instagram) are after working hours, let the person making the shoutout know that that is your preferred time. If they do not like you calling the shots, let it be, after all a mention by such people at any time can have measurable results.

How to Get Famous Instagrammers to Promote Your Page And/ Or Products

Nowadays, renowned social media users, including famous Instagrammers, are being called influencers. These people have huge followings on their social media platforms. People who follow them are generally dedicated to the influencer's content, opinions, and ideas. Due to the difficulty in making the right purchase decision, some people depend on recommendations from friends and family. On social media, potential buyers are increasingly relying on recommendations from Instagram influencers and other social media stars. As a business or company, you can engage famous Instagrammers to promote your page and or your products.

Many people have strange beliefs when it comes to approaching an influencer for the first time. For instance, some believe that influencers approach brands rather than the other way around. What is true is that Instagram influencers make the initial decision, whether or not they embrace and market a particular brand's product or service. If they like the product or the main objective of a page, they approach the company and request to represent it.

Apparently, they promote a brand even without any direct partnership.

Even as this can and does happen, it is the companies who approach Instagram influencers about promoting their brands. They simply ask them to try to review a new product line and assess whether or not they can incorporate it into their marketing strategy. You do not need to wait for Instagram influencers to approach you because it may never happen. These are people who run on a tight schedule and may not even spare a minute to look for people. After all, they are famous, and people should find them.

Another way you can go to influential Instagrammers is by connecting through a Platform; they are obviously on every social media platform. Notably, a majority of Instagram influencers believe the best way to connect with brands is through an influencer platform. A platform gives a neutral, third-party space where influencers and brands can meet and discuss the way forward. The platform facilitates brands and discovers new and growing influencers, and vice-versa. Most of the platform is guided by terms which properly govern how both parties act. This provides some security for how business is carried out between both influencers and brands.

So, how exactly do you find influencers? The most viable way is searching through Instagram and hashtags. In addition, influencers may also be found through an influencer platform, which is usually a lot easier.

Connecting and engaging with your existing customer base may also let you know who they follow and listen to on social media. For instance, if a large number of your customers are following a particular make-up Instagrammer, connect with that person and use him or her as an influencer.

It is fair to offer incentives for Instagram influencers who promote your brand and/or product. Politely engage with them first before requesting they promote your page or product. After establishing a perfect relationship, you may offer them content or request they review products or services. In short, there is no shortage of approaches to connect with influencers to promote your brand or product.

ADVANCED STRATEGIES TO INCREASE ENGAGEMENT, GENERATING SALES & GOING VIRAL

If you use Instagram for marketing purposes, there is a high likelihood that you have noticed a decrease in Instagram engagement. Do not get worried if you are not getting as many likes, comments, or new followers as you used to. In any case, it is not just you. Perhaps, you are not engaging your followers as you should. Here are advanced strategies to help you combat the downturn in engagement, generate sales, and go viral.

Avoid Using Instagram Bots

Using Instagram bots is the same as Instagram atomization. Instagram is becoming more completive. As a result, one needs to generate continuous content and have a lot of engagement in terms of like and comments. This is difficult to keep up with and, as a result, users are using Instagram atomization. In so doing, they have left all the engagement to Instagram bots which do not have feelings and may not engage the same way humans do. To rejuvenate engagement, you must be ready to forfeit atomization and do it yourself.

Control of Content Quality

It does not matter how many Instagram tips or eBook guides you read about increasing Instagram engagement. If you do not post quality content on Instagram, chances are that you will be ruining engagement with your followers. People want content which that can be useful to their livelihood. High-quality content will help you go viral and generate sales.

MAINTAIN LONG-TERM CONNECTIONS

Believing that posting content is enough to increase engagement is wrong thinking. It is crucial to build a fan base with the aim of maintaining a long-term connection. This is a way of ensuring that your followers care about your content, too. To build a great connection, you need to be in constant communication with your followers, like and comment on their posts, tag them in your photos and watch their stories. However, remember to always be relevant in your posts. Avoid sharing spam content, as it hurts trust level and may only result in losing followers.

BE KEEN ON TRENDS

This simply means that you pay attention to the changes that happen on Instagram that can help you to increase engagement. For instance, the use of GIFs is a trend and more engaging than videos. Actually, research shows more people do not have the time to watch a long video to the end. Therefore, to engage more with such an audience, you need to give them shorter video formats – GIFs.

THE SECRET WEAPON... VIDEOS

You must have noticed how much people use videos in their marketing strategy, especially on Instagram. They have understood the benefits that come with using videos as a marketing tool. Many businesses are discovering the power of using video in their Instagram marketing strategy. Actually, more companies are realizing that video has become one of the most highly shared content formats on the Internet, and can foster their marketing strategy. What makes videos secret weapons in converting social media followers into customers and increasing sales?

VIDEOS CONVEY INFORMATION MORE EFFICIENTLY

When trying to find out more about a product or service, there is a tendency to know the details quickly. Preferably, in an easy-to-process presentation which contains all details but compressed together. Videos are excellent ways to communicate with existing and potential customers. In just a few seconds, you can grab their attention and explain what your business is about and why they should consider your products or services. Even though this can be done through writing, the best way of doing it faster and in a more memorable way is by creating a video.

CREATING BRAND AWARENESS

Using videos improves the connection between your brand, customers, and the message you intend to convey. For this reason, it is imperative to create a clear, entertaining, and relevant story, because a video can immensely increase brand association.

VIDEO IS MEASURABLE

With present technology, one is able to measure the profitability and effectiveness of marketing tools used in marketing strategy. Analytics are readily available and can be very helpful in evaluating how useful videos are in marketing. Figures from an ROI analysis can help in making appealing videos as well as steering your marketing strategy in the right direction.

VIDEO REVEALS PERSONALITY

The most effective social media marketers reach their audiences by being unique. This uniqueness can send out a personality trait that the audience will have about you. Simple videos speak a lot when it comes to what one stands for. Even more, they show your traits, personality, and how you conduct business.

VIDEO WILL BOOST SOCIAL MEDIA ENGAGEMENT

Social media platform, particularly Instagram, places a high priority on video content because they know it is what users want. Do we not like sharing content that will entertain our friends and arouse their happy feeling? Videos have a better chance of doing that and can make customers happy. Unlike links, images, and plain text, a video has a better chance of gaining shared followers. This makes Instagram livelier and engagement is increased.

HOW TO WRITE CAPTIONS THAT GET YOUR FOLLOWERS TO DO WHAT YOU WANT

Using Instagram to increase product sale volumes is beyond uploading a great photo or video. A caption is equally as vital as your Instagram photo or video itself! With Instagram having grown into a huge marketing platform, it is absolutely important to know how to motivate your audience to buy your products. You can do that using captions. Below are tips on how you should write to influence your followers.

Avoid Overusing Hashtags

Many marketers and influencers are witnesses that hashtags have proven to be a great way to find new followers. Nevertheless, you must be careful while using them. If you use too many hashtags, you will only experience the opposite effect. Rather than getting more followers, you will only push them away. You should know that it looks like a desperate attempt to get new followers, this is definitely not what you want for your brand.

PAY ATTENTION TO YOUR WRITING STYLE

Instagram users enjoy following pages, Users that have a specific attractive writing style. For example, can add timestamps to your posts. Alternatively, you can be even deeper and choose to use short captions or more like storytelling captions. It is wise to test to notice the reactions of existing followers and start using a specific style afterward.

CREATE A CALL-TO-ACTION IN YOUR INSTAGRAM CAPTION

The simple act of creating a call-to-action in your Instagram caption will lead to more engagement in your posts. Additionally, inviting your audience to comment or engage can go a long way when it comes to engaging with followers. Even with this being said, avoid including a call-to-action in all Instagram captions. Creating a perfect good call-to-action is a great way to inspire your followers to engage with your business both inside and outside of Instagram.

USE EMOJIS IN YOUR INSTAGRAM CAPTION

Even as you do not intend to use emojis to draw attention to your call-to-action, use them to add personality to your Instagram caption. To make a perfect caption, you can insert multiple emojis at the beginning. It will catch the eye of your followers with a bit of creativity, so they want to click to read more. Otherwise, you can replace whole words with an emoji.

ADD HASHTAGS TO INSTAGRAM CAPTIONS

It is important to note that you would be selling yourself with Instagram captions. For this reason, use the right hashtags to help you extend to a wider audience. Additionally, hashtags will make visible to more potential clients and help you grow your following and later to an increased sales volume.

Chapter 6: Converting Followers into Buyers

How to Create Links That Produce Clicks

Currently, there is a new feature called Instagram Link which allows users to create a link in and story images. In the past, Instagram only allowed users to insert a link in the bio of your profile. So, why not take advantage of it to show all your posts in a clickable way? This way, you will definitely generate images that can guide you to a product page, publication or any specific landing page. Here is how to create that produce clicks.

1) First, tap the camera icon to begin your story. Take several photos or shoot a video or swipe up to select an image or video from your camera roll. The video or image selected has to be no longer than 24 hours created the visual to qualify as a story.

2) Click on the Link Icon – (an icon that looks like a chain link at the top of the screen). Ideally, the icon only appears if you have not less than

10000 followers to your business account. Add the URL of the link that you would like to add to your images or videos. After adding the URL, click on done.

3) Add a call to action. Ensure that you edit your story before tapping on the "Add Your Story" icon, and then add a call to action. In case you add a clickable link to a photo, it will be visible on the screen before the next story pops up. The clickable link is not easily noticeable and may be easy to miss. Therefore, include a "see more" text link to make it noticeable. A perfect call to action must include something like "swipe up to see our latest product" or simply some luring words that will propel your audience to click.

4) Add the content to the story and you are done.

BENEFITS OF USING LINKS IN INSTAGRAM

Using links in your Instagram posts can be of immeasurable benefits. Probably, you may have a idea about what benefits you may experience when you use links. However, just to make it clear, here are a few benefits.

It leads to an increase in traffic to your website or blog from Instagram. It goes without being said that adding links to your Instagram content will lead to an increase in the number of people being redirected to your website.

Improve sales by redirecting buyers to the product page, making it easy for potential buyers to view more details and make a purchase decision.

It helps you measure the effectiveness of your Instagram strategy. If you are a social media manager, marketer or influencer, you want to show your clients you have plenty of followers. In addition, it is necessary to let them know that your strategies will help to boost their sales.

HOW TO CREATE DIGITAL PRODUCTS TO SELL ON INSTAGRAM

Having created digital products, you need to come up with the right strategy of selling to potential and existing customers. This implies coming up with a plan of making sure that your audience will, in fact, buy your digital product. The following steps will help you to prevent the unnecessary costs and disappointment in making a product no one wants.

TALK TO POTENTIAL BUYERS

It is crucial to ensure that potential buyers are people you trust. Most potential customers are most avid, engaged readers of your Instagram posts and stories. Individually message at least three of them with your value proposition and ask them for their honest opinion. Other than messaging, you can also contact them through email. Embrace their criticism and adjust your idea accordingly.

CREATE CONTENT AROUND THE IDEA

Create a buzz for your product and gauge audience reaction before you make the product. Basically, you can begin with some blog posts around your product that will be introduced to your readers and incite curiosity. Further, you can take questions and comments about the product and use them to improve your initial product idea.

CREATE YOUR MINIMUM VIABLE PRODUCT

A minimum viable product does not translate to a half-finished product. It implies a complete product that is a fraction of the scale of the digital product you are creating. A great approach to envision this is using the cake model. For instance, if you are planning to produce an entire album of digital background songs, you can release one song first.

Additionally, you can write a summary of it first if you are planning to sell it as an e-book.

CREATE A SALES PAGE FOR THE PRODUCT.

It seems unwise to jump the gun and create a sales page for something you have not yet created. However, what you want to sell here is your free minimum viable product. You can also offer an additional discount to individuals who take the trouble to fill out a feedback form about the minimum viable product you intend to release out there. Ensure taking back the feedback constructively and make use it to build a better and more useful product.

SELLING PHYSICAL AND DIGITAL PRODUCTS ON INSTAGRAM

In the current business world, sellers are able to sell their physical and digital products. When it comes to selling physical goods, sellers give their physical address so that buyers can visit their stores to make a purchase. However, selling digital products only need a medium of money transfer. In this case, the customer makes the payment online and the seller sends the product, through the internet. The following are some on the digital products that may be sold on Instagram.

E-BOOKS

Nowadays, people just cannot get enough eBooks on their e-reader, tablets, or even smartphones. You can now access information whenever and wherever is just irresistible. It does not necessarily have to be a traditionally long eBook to be valuable and sellable. It depends on the niche you are in. However, concise manuals, reports, case studies, white papers, checklists, and anything else that is informative is always valuable to the right reader. Therefore, you should already have a head start in understanding what category of information is important to your audience.

eCOURSES/WEBINARS

Teaching more complicated topics that can be presented in an eBook may require Videos. More importantly, videos allow you to connect with your audience on a different level. eCourses are different to Webinars. Webinars are conducted live on a previously scheduled time, while eCourses are pre-recorded, on-demand training lessons. Obviously, you can compile webinars on the most suitable topics and bundle them as an eCourse later.

Nevertheless, the slides should be part of the package when you offer your buyers an eCourse.

AUDIO COURSES

Audio courses have conventionally been utilized for teaching languages. Nowadays, you can create an audio course about almost anything or any niche. At the end of the recorded audio, it is a good add-on later on whether or not you are planning to create an eBook or a video course to complement to the audio. Notably, an eBook can easily be converted into an audiobook or webinars into audio files that you can also sell.

WEB ELEMENTS

If you are a graphic designer, this may probably a great fit for you. People are continually looking for beautiful graphics. Graphics may be intended to be used for their blogs, corporate presentations, or just for personal projects.

MUSIC

The demand for digital music is on the rise. Everyone from YouTube vloggers to big corporate video producers are looking for suitable audio, which can be used as background music. Free is the most viable option for them. Nevertheless, most professionals are willing to pay a bit more for background music that is flawlessly produced and fits their content preferences.

PHOTOS

Presently, high-resolution photos are also in demand. People from all niches are looking for stock photos and images to use in their blog posts as visual elements. It is hard to stand out from the crowd if you are taking pictures of the usual elements. Take time and collect the best and unique photos that will make you exceptional.

Chapter 7: Converting Followers into Clients via Instagram Sales Funnel

Without proper marketing strategies, your business will eventually fail due to the lack of customers. No one out there will get to know about your business, what you are offering and where exactly they can get your products. Therefore, if you have not already put time and effort into this mission, now is the time to start. Apparently, one easy way to start is the use of a sales funnel. This strategy is so named due to the fact that this particular marketing strategy looks just like a funnel in diagram form.

Even though you may market your products or services to thousands of people, only a few will provide contact information and become leads. Out of those leads, only a fraction will become clients. Here is how to build your Instagram sales funnel that will deliver results.

Instagram Ads

Instagram ads have proved to be incredibly useful for businesses and organizations of all types and sizes when it comes to marketing. Presently, Instagram Ads are managed through the Facebook Ads Manager dashboard. This makes it easy to sync with your paid efforts on Facebook and to take advantage of the wide range of targeting options. If you can get this into a comfortable range where you make a profit on every transaction, you can scale the campaign by increasing the budget and find more success.

TURN YOUR BIO INTO A CALL TO ACTION

A profile bio is your prime real estate without so much space to post whatever you want. You must utilize the space by posting only what your audience will find useful and what will draw you closer to you and your brand. Using this space to make a compelling call-to-action is one of the things you should do when implementing Instagram sales funnels. The app does not have a lot of other space for text or links throughout its interface. For this reason, you really need to get creative and use the best of your ability.

USING USER-GENERATED CONTENT

E-commerce products work exceptionally well when driven by user-generated content. This entails using other clients to market your products to potential clients. This can go a long way in helping you to put Instagram sales to funnel into practice. Therefore, persuading followers to repost photos of your product in use, tagging your account, or using your branded hashtag. If you get influential people, you will have nailed it!

User-generated content creates a culture around your brand from real customers helps to promote awareness. Using this tactic will enable you to create an online community centered on your business, meaning that you have the full support of customers and goodwill. Reposting of user-generated photos on the business feed will further entice your audience to get involved and propel them to buy if they do not own the product. Ultimately, you will develop a continuous engagement, increase your brand's visibility and convert most of your followers into clients.

JOIN FORCES WITH INFLUENCERS

With the right strategy, your brand can settle on a strategic partnership with a renowned influencer. Ensure that you generate and keenly assess a great return on investment in terms of conversions and brand awareness. Working with influencers will enable you to leverage a network and brand to bring awareness to your e-commerce offerings. You will benefit to your success and popularity.

This method of disseminating your marketing message will not feel like an advertisement because the message will be coming from the influencer's personal and authentic voice. Followers continue to welcome endorsements from trusted Instagram stars and influencers, amidst tightening restrictions on sponsored content transparency.

LINK IN STORY

This feature is only available to accounts with more than 10,000 Instagram followers. This is all the more reason to prioritize Instagram and start building that audience to benefits from this feature. Users with such accounts are eligible to include links in Instagram stories. Instagram stories go a long way in giving a business more space to implement their sales funnel. One is not limited to suing such a short description as in a bio. Therefore, one can make use of this space to convert more followers into clients in more words, maybe benefits of owning a given product.

INSTAGRAM AUTOMATION

In reference to Instagram's terms and conditions, users should not apply Instagram automation whatsoever. Even so, it is a stable and efficient way to grow the followers' base, if done in the right way. There is a high likelihood of being banned if noticed to be using Instagram automation. However, with current technology and tools, you can hide your tracks and make it increasingly challenging for Instagram to detect.

Instagram automation tools are meant to mimic human behavior in terms of using Instagram functions. For instance, there are automation settings to delay intervals for every like, follow, or unfollow. Even more, there is a function to randomize the actions of the Instagram bot similar to what a human would.

Exactly where should one apply Instagram automation? Instagram automation should only be used in performing the following tasks.

- Likes – one can use Instagram automation to automatically, like posts with specific tags, from particular people, and many more.

- Follow – this is the use of the automation function to find and follow Instagram profiles by tags, followers of specific accounts, those who commented or liked particular posts, and many more.

- Unfollow – this is the use of Instagram automation to unfollow Instagram profiles after a certain amount of time, or if they have not followed you back.

- Posting – one can use Instagram automation to activate the ability to post photos, add captions, and post stories automatically.

- Comments – automating this means that creating a function with the ability to automatically comment on photos with specific tags, from particular people, and many more.

- Direct Messages – this is simply the ability to send direct messages to users who newly followed you, an entire follower base, or Instagram influencers you want to engage with.

The best way to make sure that you do not get banned for using Instagram automation is making it difficult for Instagram administrators to notice your automated functions. But how do you do that? You can do this in three ways.

- Do not use Instagram automation for a continuous and lengthy period.

- Do not automate everything, because there are specific tasks that will draw attention to your account if it looks like spam. Experts recommend that you only use Instagram automation for posting, following, unfollowing, and liking photos.

- Do not automate direct messaging.

- Do not automate comments. The major problem with automating comments is that all you will have one common comment that will apply to a wide variety of photos.

As a disclaimer, there is always a huge risk of getting banned on Instagram for using automation tools. It is imperative to note that automation is not a single solution to growing your Instagram following. However, automation may have a substantial growth by when done correctly.

Always use it cautiously and do not be solely dependent on automation to grow your followers. Go through the following tips on how you can get more than 10K followers on Instagram. Take time to assess what you can embrace and implement it to the latter.

CHAPTER 8: ROAD TO 10K FOLLOWERS IN A MONTH

HOW TO GET MORE THAN 10K FOLLOWERS IN A MONTH

When starting out on Instagram, it is exciting to imagine how many followers your account can get out of over 1 billion users. The truth is that your first 10,000 Instagram followers are the hardest to get. The main reason behind this is that no one knows who you are yet. You still have to go a long way to prove yourself as a successful brand and influencers. However, this does not necessarily imply that it is not possible. Having a huge number of followers within a short period is possible, provided you carry on as required. Below are tips to that will help you hit 10,000 Instagram followers within a month.

SELECT A THEME AND ADHERE TO IT

Selecting a theme for your Instagram page is a great way to appeal to a niche community. Even better, you can just make a unique name for yourself. Besides, themes can also compel Instagram users to decide to follow you. If they know that you publish consistent and similar content to the picture or post they originally discover, it makes it an easy decision to click 'follow.' In case that one post liked by your audience was just a one-off on your feed, most people among your audience will move on to explore other pages instead.

JOIN INSTAGRAM ENGAGEMENT GROUPS

Are you simply beginning to get followers on Instagram? This strategy is best for beginners. A few Instagram newbies have watched their Instagram followers increase faster than they expected, such that everyone remain asking what they did differently. The fact is that they joined engagement groups.

While it may be difficult to join the biggest Instagram engagement groups, you will get a more targeted list of Instagram followers by sticking to your niche. You can easily find Instagram engagement groups for travel, beauty, fashion amongst other niches. From these groups, you can obtain followers and likes from people who have similar interests as you. However, if you are serious about getting the attention, then you should also return the favor by following fan pages for people who will join the group.

Even if it may not help with immediate sales, it helps your brand gain credibility beforehand. It is important to note that is a short-term strategy. It should be used for getting Instagram followers only in the first few weeks on Instagram and not in the long-term.

CHOOSING THE RIGHT INSTAGRAM CONTENT

To achieve a huge following of real people on Instagram, you have to produce content. It should not only be made specifically for Instagram but also the right fit for what your audience wants. While creating the content, finding the right approach and style is crucial. This is because your content will become the way your followers recognize you.

Generally, there are several types of images that work well with a lot of niches. Posters with inspirational or humorous quotes, quality food photography, or scenic images are safe starting points in your content creation strategy. It is wise to carefully consider what type of content you are producing. Always recognize that Instagram is a hit because it is a wholly unique platform. It provides a user experience that is completely different than something like other social media platforms. In short, come up with unique content for your Instagram account.

Produce Content Your Audience Will Love

When you comprehend what type of content is right for your brand, it is time to really focus on making extraordinary posts that you know will connect with your audience. This may appear obvious but content creation itself has been neglected by many marketers and influencers. Discover what your clients appreciate seeing on Instagram or what themes resonate with them. Afterward, you can go on and populate your account with relevant content.

Whatever the case, you have to connect with your audience. Do not forget the saying that beauty is in the eye of the beholder. That is why it is so important to build up a good relationship with your audience and learn what type of content they like. There have been various occasions people, which have posted something that we thought would totally increase engagement. To their surprise, it is turned out to be a dud.

One way to ensure you produce excellent content is finding out what your competition is posting. Moreover, take note of what kind of imagery used on their websites or blogs that are popular in your industry and emulate. Do not copy and paste!

Ask Customers to Share their Photos

When you are just beginning an Instagram marketing strategy, getting followers on Instagram will be much easier with customer photos in your feed, it goes a long way in helping to increase social proof.

On the off chance that you have just had a couple of sales, reach out to customers and offer a free gift or cash incentive for taking quality images using the product they purchased. Obviously, giving incentives should not be a long-term strategy, but for the short-term. It is meant to help you grow as you try to build your brand. As more customers start viewing customer photos on your Instagram, they will naturally start tagging you in posts when they obtain their products. If you post a comment on their post, repost the content and follow them, you are likely to lure them to follow back.

HAVE A CONSISTENT STYLE

This sounds like one of those insufficient approaches to gain followers on Instagram. However, this is not the case. Experts in social media marketing believe that people do not follow a page because of the content posted. However, they follow a page because of what they think the future content will be like. What they expect in the future is consistency in the style of content that makes them arouse at the moment.

Getting used to a consistent style is more than just branding. It is also about creating anticipation for your Instagram account that your followers or potential followers can count on. They preferably want to see more of the same type of style content, every day. Once you are able to deliver that consistency with every post, you will grow your followers on Instagram at a faster rate over a short period of time.

USE INSTAGRAM POSTS IN BLOG POSTS

If you own a personal or business blog, you can insert your Instagram pictures into your blog posts. For instance, if you are in the fashion niche, you might write a blog post about styling tips. You can pick posts from Instagram where you show pictures of your layered outfits or a trendy outfit look. To do all this, go onto the Instagram website on your desktop, go to your page, click the post, click the '...' icon and click Embed. Then, copy that link into your blog post's code section.

After some time, more individuals will visit your blog and will probably look at your Instagram account as well. This is more of a long-term game, particularly if you are not getting traffic. Adding your Instagram posts from the start gives you a higher chance of visibility and you will really start seeing massive returns within time.

FOLLOW PEOPLE WHO LIKE COMPETING PAGES

To get that desired increment in the number of Instagram followers, you need to find people who follow brands who are your competitors. Who are your greatest rivals on Instagram on the actual market? Write them down and peruse their posts to see who is commenting on their posts. This will help you know their preference, follow them and engage with them.

Remember that it is better to go for the smaller brands while picking competitors on Instagram. This is justifiable because if you were selling makeup brushes and trying to get people who comment on nail polish, there is a good chance that they are not the right audience despite being in a similar niche. Notably, bigger brands tend to have more customer loyalty. As you keep engaging and following people who follow a competitor, you will certainly start to gather a strong following of your own.

TREASURE YOUR INSTAGRAM FOLLOWERS

One of the greatest errors people make when building their Instagram account is valuing their followers as numbers. Followers are not by any means the only metric that matters when it comes to Instagram. However, you can get fixated in growing the follower count that you fail to appreciate that each person who chooses to follow you is actually a living, breathing human being. Remember, it does not make a difference what sort of account you are running, whether it is personal or business. The same is true everywhere; just do not relent treating your followers like gold.

WORK WITH INFLUENCERS

Another approach to get an increase in the number of Instagram followers is by getting influencer shout outs or having influencers do an account takeover. An influencer has already existing loyal following and can give you a shout out that will result in a few new followers for your account and possibly a few sales. Before engaging an influencer, be ready to write up a contract that prohibits the influencer from sending fake traffic. Note that when you get a sudden rush of fake follower on your account, you risk getting your account banned.

POST REGULARLY

Intend to post on a regular basis, maybe, about once every three to four hours. However, avoid bulk posting a whole bunch of photos in one sitting. This makes users start regarding your posts as spam and unfollow you. Actually, think of it as sowing seeds. You do not want to just put all your seeds into a hole in one go, you want to spread them out. The best practices indicate that one opt for consistency. If your audience cannot comfortably rely on you to post regularly, you will not find many people willing to follow you on the off chance that will post something every now and then.

HOST GIVEAWAYS

You might be able to get more followers if you host giveaways on Instagram and have a small audience. However, if you host giveaways on your website and incorporate an option to follow you on Instagram, you will have a much bigger reach. If your audience is small, you can go on to post your giveaway in certain Facebook groups or on giveaway blogs.

If you are just starting out, giveaways can enable you to get more followers on Instagram. Be aware that if you do them too often, you probably will not get the type of audience you want. If the goal is to get sales, giveaways will not necessarily help you get more customers. Nevertheless, this strategy can work quite well if you are only looking to get Instagram followers fast.

MASS ENGAGE

In order to gain more followers, you must engage with more people on Instagram. To find the best accounts to engage with, search them and hashtags relevant to your brand. Utilize Liking, commenting, and following to increase your engagement with followers. At the moment, Instagram only allows you to follow up to 7,500 people. So, take advantage of that! When you engage with accounts which have similar traits and interests as yours, they are more interested in following you and engaging in your posts. To avoid your account from being banned, you must make sure you are engaging within Instagram's limits, such as 300-350 likes/hour, 8-14 comments/hour, 20-40 follows/hour, 20-40 unfollows/hour.

Most experts recommend beginning with not as much as the numbers above for at least 2-3 weeks before testing Instagram limits on your page. In case you reach one of Instagram's limits, you will be restricted from using the particular feature for the next 24 hours. If this continues to happen, your account could be shut down permanently.

USE HASHTAGS

Hashtags (keywords preceded by "#" symbol) might seem like something only annoying teenagers use. However, that is not the case. They are ways for followers and other Instagram users to easily navigate through to topics they're interested in. Including #hashtags to your image enables your content to be found more easily by those who do not already follow you.

To start with, explore the most well-known hashtags, and then compile them. In some cases, this involves building a tremendous list of keywords that are relevant to a specific niche and what the used images generally are about.

So, how can one get the most appropriate hashtags?

- Check out what the top-trending hashtags are with Tags for Likes to find hashtags relevant to your niche.

- Copy the hashtags that the top influencers in your niche are utilizing. Use this as an approach to not only generate more exposure and gain more followers but as a way of getting on the radars of other influencers.

NEGOTIATE TO GET SHOUTOUTS

With regards to growing an immense following on Instagram, you will need to accustom yourself to the idea of collaboration over competition. This is where the incredibly powerful concept of shout outs and S4S comes into play. Just to mention, S4S stands for "share for share." If you are looking forward to gaining a million followers on Instagram, you need to get used to sharing other people's content.

The basics of using shout outs is quite simple. You just request an influencer in your niche if they would like to share your content and you will consequently share theirs. This way, you will have the capacity to uncover each other's brands to each other's audiences. This is how you get in touch to some of whom likely have never even heard of you in the past. In the event that you pick who you do S4S with precisely, you will most likely discover someone with an audience who you know will like your content too. You will rapidly find out that one of the biggest aspects of Instagram is that it enables you to tap directly into a niche with distinct likes, interests, hobbies, and needs.

USE APPS TO INCREASE INSTAGRAM FOLLOWERS

When most people first start building their Instagram account, they use a bot - an app to increase Instagram followers. In most cases, they are also called Instagress. It works really well at first and allows users to easily build up the first few thousand Instagram followers. Eventually, they stop using the bots because they are of no use after gaining the needed following. Unfortunately, Instagress and other apps, which are used to increase Instagram followers, usually get shut down after getting noticed by Instagram administrators. Actually, an account may be banned from using such applications. Even as they can deliver followers, the risk just is not worth it.

REPOST OTHER PEOPLE'S CONTENT

Some people build their Instagram account entirely by using a strategy revolving around reposting other people's content. The best way to do this without getting flagged for plagiarism is to credit and acknowledging the original poster in your description at all time. Instagram's terms and conditions requires one to ask for permission before reposting.

USE INSIGHTS

It very easy to track your followers' and post's impressions on Instagram. In the event that you are looking to gain a large number of followers on Instagram, make sure you switch your personal page to a business profile so you can track your insights. Once switched, you can use the information available to know the prime time to make your postings. By doing this, you will get the most engagement which will, in turn, gain you more followers.

USE GEOTAGS AND TAG BRANDS

Most notably, an Instagram geotag is similar to a check-in on Facebook. Many people will look at prominent posts in their region, and therefore adding a location to your posts is a great way for targeted accounts to see your posts. Along with geotags, tagging brands and large accounts gives your post the opportunity to been seen by a huge mass of followers.

Perhaps there are other ways you can use to get more than 10K followers in a month. You should not rule them out. Rather, combine them with what is discussed above to get more results.

Chapter 9: Social Media Principles and Social Media Myths

Principles of Social Media

If you are a social media marketer of influencer, chances are you must have recognized that the prevailing task is one of the most challenging jobs in making a brand visible and profitable. The sheer depth to the task is immense because of the changes to the things that need to be managed on a continuous basis. Additionally, as much as it is a dream come true to any marketer, getting it right may be a difficult endeavor. To make it easier, there are a set of peculiar principles to follow if you want to fully benefit.

Have a Robust Strategy Beforehand

Some businesses and brands decide to launch a campaign only to realize not too far into it that they either lack enough content to sustain momentum or they have no idea about the campaign. This is just one of the countless issues that needs to be addressed before dipping your toes in the social media waters. Additionally, other concerns that need to be attended are branding, lead generation, public relations (PR) and Search Engine Optimization (SEO). One ought to understand what exactly their marketing objectives are, who their audience is, and how better results can be achieved.

BE PERSISTENT AND PATIENT

If you are a growing brand and have a negligible following, be patient and know that it will take time to get success. The fact is that attention to your account is earned and not given on a silver platter. Even if you opt to use boosted content, it will still take time. You will need a pervasive, bona fide presence on social media to be taken seriously. In social media, customers and potential clients are more likely to respond affirmatively to what you have to offer the more you engage with them.

TREASURE YOUR AUDIENCE AND TREAT THEM RIGHT

Always remember that you never get a second chance to make a great first impression. Therefore, treat the members of your audience like VIPs. Express gratitude toward them for following you and regularly ask how you can help them. Additionally, speak to their needs and interests, give them credit, and praise them when you can. Take time to show them how much you value the time they take to watch, listen and learn from you. Give them far more attention than they are giving to you, and chances are that your welcome and warmth will be reciprocated.

BE AVAILABLE, REMAIN RESPONSIVE AND ENGAGING

Fortunately, social media has made it possible for you to engage with your followers in real time and at any time. However, the bad news is that they can contact you at their very own comfort. The general expectation is that you will respond to them immediately to raise an issue. Banker's hours, nights, weekends, and lunchtime are unheard-of when it comes to social media. Managing a social media campaign means you should be a hands-on person, no matter what your schedule is in real life. While using any of the social media platforms, you should be there for your audience at a moment's notice. If you snooze, you will definitely lose. In social media, there is neither time for laxity nor rest for the weary.

DEMONSTRATE THE HUMAN SIDE OF YOUR BRAND

One of the greatest mistakes committed by marketers, influencers, and professionals is to underestimate the significance of the social in social media. People do business with individuals who are willing to engage as humans and not logos behind a litany of promotional messages and corporate gobbledygook. As you do this, be kind, generous, and naturally social. Never forget that unfriendly and contrived content will get you nowhere on social media. Sincerity and spontaneity will keep you on top of your competitors.

DISCOVER HOW TO BE EFFICIENT

Presently, social media is altogether a different place compared to how it was just a few years ago. There are a number of different tools and platforms to help you automate your work as a social media marketer or influencer. With so much help available, it can seem overwhelming or even counterproductive to join a million platforms and then watch as you get busy doing nothing. Just select only one medium and capitalize on it.

PERFECT QUALITY CONTROL

With such a large space on social media to make an impact, it is easy to go astray at times. Many brands suffer as they start to spread themselves too thin and then lower the quality of the content they post. As a good rule of thumb, it is always imperative to focus on quality content above everything else. This is a key principle because it directs the majority of your work as a social media marketer or influencer. This implies that you should make quality control a guiding principle before you focus on anything else. Obviously, everything integrates with the voice your brand has. In any case, the minute a brand gets messy and conflicting with quality, it turns out to be hard to recover. As a social media manager, a marketer or influencer, it is your job to always ensure high-quality content.

APPLY THE PARETO PRINCIPLE.

Applying the Pareto Principle means that you will yield 80 percent of your results with 20 percent of input. This implies that media platforms should be up to 20 percent promotional and the remaining 80 percent should be directly linked to customer issues. It would be prudent to create an "audience profile" for your modest customers. Utilize demographic data provided by the social media platforms concerning age, gender, income, and education level to identify the needs of your audience and the prevailing preference trends. Further, determine what makes your audience motivated to follow you and do not relent to make it count in every post.

BE CUSTOMER ORIENTED

Customers are progressively hoping to get a quality customer service experience when dealing with any business person via social media. By providing such an experience, it will allow customers to interact with representatives via a platform that they are familiar with. Push marketing on social media is proving to be less successful than it has been in the past. This may partially be due to infrastructure changes in social networks, and the growing maturity of the customer's usage. Therefore, be customer oriented in everything you do on social media. After all, any display of careless attitude to your customers may cost you greatly.

Be Professional

Social media engagement and community management is a specialized field that has rapidly grown and developed over the past ten years. The professional application of social media and community concepts is a distinct capability that requires training, experience, and professionalism. This is Regardless of the accessibility of using social media for personal use or for business purposes.

Data is Everything

It is astonishing that this principle is still not a concern for social media managers, marketers, and influencers. Data should be the cornerstone of all the marketing work that you do. It is essential to have data about how your social media campaigns are performing as well as the historical context of each campaign. Generally speaking, social media marketers need quick and efficient data to help them to make right decisions. Further, overall social media management needs to have momentum which needs to be consistent to help the business to stay on top of trends and to increase profitability.

IT IS NOT JUST A SLICE OF THE MARKETING PIE

All the well-meaning marketers might make you believe that social networking platforms are nothing more than an additional platform to distribute their message to the masses. Well, it isn't true, and if that's what you think, then you will end up as social media road kill. The idea of social media is to familiarize the audience with your brand and to increase your reach. If all you do on Instagram is talk about yourself and use it as a place to make your sales pitch, it will do you more harm than good.

SO-CALLED SOCIAL MEDIA EXPERTS

These days, everyone and anyone claims to be a social media expert. These so-called experts are sprouting out of nowhere. They can certainly talk the talk, but they can't walk the walk. Someone can claim to be an authority only when such a person has years of productivity, a good reputation, and can produce quantifiable results. So, you don't really need to hire a social media expert. That's just a trap you should beware of.

SOME THINGS NEVER CHANGE

In recent times, the world of marketing has undergone a tremendous change, but the good old-fashioned rules about communication, PR, and marketing still hold true. These basic ethics will never go out of fashion. It is important to know your target audience, the value you can add to their lives, and the purpose you serve. You need to consider all this if you want to develop a good marketing strategy. Also, it will do you good to understand that social media is only a small part of your marketing strategy and not your entire strategy. So, don't stray from these values when you consider the option of social media marketing. If you want your social media marketing campaign to be successful, then there are various elements that need to be put together. All the elements of your campaign need to be in complete harmony with one other. Social media is just an element of your campaign and you need to make all the other elements work together. You must use the traditional methods of marketing and integrate it with your social media campaign.

SOCIAL MEDIA IS NOT JUST RESTRICTED TO FACEBOOK OR INSTAGRAM

Facebook, Instagram, Twitter, and LinkedIn are amongst the most popular social media sites, but they account for only a part of the ecosystem of social media. Web forums, email lists, user groups, various photo and video sharing services, podcasts, social bookmarking sites, and niche online communities are all part of social media. You need to keep in mind that you will have to try to understand the turf that your customers use to socialize, and you need to involve yourself in those platforms as well.

Most brands tend to gradually distance themselves from destination websites and are instead focusing on community building strategies and plans. For building your brand, you need to concentrate on other things as well. It is a good move to have established your brand on various social media outposts such as LinkedIn, Facebook, and even

Twitter, but you need to remember that your existing and potential customers might actually be active on various other social media platforms and affinity groups apart from the ones mentioned above.

CREATE AND MAINTAIN RELATIONSHIPS

Marketing is all about building and then maintaining relationships. Social media provides you with the tools and the platform that you require to fulfill this purpose. However, it does not mean that you must completely ignore the basic, personal form of communication that is important for being successful. You need to understand that technology is as important as a personal connection when it comes to social media marketing.

DON'T GET CARRIED AWAY BY SOCIAL MEDIA

You need to understand that social media can help you do a lot of things but not everything. You have to put in considerable time and effort if you want to be able to make your marketing strategy work. If you do your bit while you use social media platforms, then you will be able to reach your goals.

It Is Not All About the Return on Relationship

You must be able to gauge your success by making use of both qualitative and quantitative metrics as well. It is important to concentrate on brand recognition, reputation in the market, and awareness, but metrics such as the money raised, increase in the number of attendees, subscribers, and even widgets sold are important. It will give you an idea of how well your business is doing. You need to be able to track the changes in the results that have been generated with the help of social media marketing. Only when you can do this will you be able to make the required changes to your campaign. You need to be able to quantify the results that have been generated.

It Is All About Being Sociable

At the end of the day, there is one thing that you need to understand. You need to be sociable. Social media is all about being sociable! No one wants to associate themselves with someone who is not sociable or just keeps on broadcasting. You need to figure out a way in which your brand seems more socially appealing to others.

Social Media Myths

There are myths that surround almost everything that happens on the surface of the earth. Even though the myths are baseless, they sometimes sound so true to be a hoax. Many of us also have a lot of biased ideas about social media which are not actually true. For this reason, it is prudent to explain the myths about social media that ought to be debunked right away.

You Need to Utilize All Social Media Platforms

A vast majority of marketers and influencers believe that a far-reaching marketing campaign is impossible without spreading it through all social media channels. Although this is not wrong, it is unnecessary. However, social networks that would be adopted depending on where your target groups are, your forecasted budget, and campaigns. Often, it is better to focus more effort on one or two platforms if limited on money and time. Otherwise, there will be high chances that content may not be personalized to fit each platform. The bottom line is, if your clientele is not using Twitter, for example, why should you waste your time trying to be present in social media platforms. It is important to evaluate and discover the most rampantly used platform among your clients and followers.

SOCIAL MEDIA Marketing CAN DO IT ALL

Today, we cannot argue that social media is not amongst the most important modes of marketing. However, it does not mean that it is the only channel you should use in your marketing endeavors. Is will only fulfill its potential in coordinating other elements of proper meriting, such as branding, influencer marketing, and Search Engine Optimization (SEO). This implies that social media should be part of your marketing strategy and not the only marketing strategy. In a nutshell, an effort should be made to use social media marketing, but a decent portion of other marketing modes should feature as well.

MOST CUSTOMERS ARE NOT ONLINE

This is a common notion by business owners and company decision makers who usually believe that their consumers cannot be found online. This myth is especially common with B2B business models who think that social media is redundant in their industry. In fact, most people who use social media to market and gain clients online have confirmed that this is wrong thinking. There are more than 2 billion people on Facebook, more than 320 million users on Twitter and about 1 million users on Instagram. With such statistics, it is unwise to believe that your audience is not using digital media in this era.

THERE IS NOTHING TO POST ABOUT

Having nothing to post on social media is just an excuse of the lazy and goalless. In the present world, you cannot lack something to post on your social media account. You have a lot of items to choose from ranging from marketing trends, trending celebrity news, fashion news, sports, and entertainment news, amongst others. Even with a vast range of items to post about, do not forget that what you post should always be aligned with your niche. Instagram marketers and influencers post only 2 posts about the brand and all the rest is related to their industry. If you do not find the trending items catchy and appropriate to your audience, be unique by offering opinions and advice on related topics. In most cases, think less about selling your product and instead aim at providing your followers with something valuable. Assess what the audience is interested in and start posting content around this. You can maybe look at what your competitors are posting for insights.

YOU NEED A HASHTAG FOR EVERY POST

We cannot rule out the fact that hashtags are essential when it comes to social media postings. While it is reasonable to think that several hashtags will bring more reach and influence, you do not need a hashtag in every post. Actually, hashtags do not really contribute to the number of followers one has in any social media platform including Instagram. It only enhances how easy your followers can find your content. A number of studies have revealed that popular posts tend to made of quality communication and not quantity!

SOCIAL MEDIA PLATFORMS OFFER FREE MARKETING

Many people believe that social media marketing is completely free of charge. In theory, it is true, but it is not the case in reality. Social media algorithms are making it increasingly difficult for brand content to be seen by all followers and other users. This has forced companies to enter a "pay to play" zone. This is the reason why social media ads spend over 15 million dollars every year. You should know renowned social media marketers and influencers pay for sponsored or boosted content. This is the surest way that your content will get propagated to as many users as possible.

SOCIAL MEDIA MARKETING WILL HARDLY DELIVER RESULTS

People who use social media for marketing purposes are not sure how to calculate social media return on investment (ROI). This is the major cause of the myth that using social media as a marketing tool does not deliver tangible results. However, more than 70 percent of marketers who know how to assess the ROI can confirm that using social media in their marketing strategy has substantial benefits.

YOU SHOULD IGNORE NEGATIVE FEEDBACK

Social media is similar to a spectator sport. It is not about making the upset customer happy. Rather, it is all about making sure your brand is well known and caring to its client. This is because thousands of other customers and prospects are looking on with a bowl of popcorn in their laps. Ideally, it is important to answer every comment positively or negatively, and do it fast. This way, you will demonstrate to everyone that you are ready to address any issue that you have regarding your product or services. Take negative feedback as a chance to correct the mistakes that would make you lose customers.

SOCIAL MEDIA COMMUNICATION WILL KILL EMAIL

This is a myth that makes most people think that communicating on any social media platform will kill emailing. Given that you must make official communication on email, the chances of killing emailing is negligible. Typically, you can never stop using email, especially when dealing with clients who like being formal. Evidently, both email and social media may be used to keep your brand top-of-mind among people who have given you the permission to do so. Thus, social media and email are complementary tactics, not conflicting.

Well, these are not the only myths about social media out there. Do not fall into anything exaggerated or understated concerning social media. If in doubt of anything about social media, the best thing is to get advice from an expert.

SOCIAL MEDIA IS A SALES TOOL

If you are overly promotional on a social media platform, then it will be a turn off for the audience. It is a general misconception that social media is a giant sounding board for brands to pitch their products and services. Well, take a moment and think about your personal usage of social media. Do you open your Facebook profile or Instagram page to check ads? Everyone uses social media to socialize and find content that is interesting. So, it is not a good idea to promote yourself too much on social media. After all, the idea is to attract customers and not turn them away. There is a simple fix to this problem. You need to make sure that the content you post is a mix of promotional and non-promotional content. The ideal ratio of non-promotional content to posts with call-to-action is 80:20.

I Need to Use Facebook, Because Everyone Does

If you try to use social media without a good marketing strategy, then all that you do is generate noise. So, why do you want to use a particular social media platform? Your answer must not be, "I have to use it, because everyone seems to be using it." If this is your answer, then you will find yourself in a world of trouble. You cannot set up a social media account and then not have an idea about what you want to post. Don't use social media because your friends, competitors, or someone else says it's a good tactic. You need to take a look at your business goals and what you plan to achieve with the help of social media. Make a list of your goals and then see if social media fits into all this.

The Audience Will Automatically Pour In

You need to understand that your audience will not immediately flock to you because you are on social media. Creating a social media account or writing a blog is not sufficient to attract people to follow or read the content you post. You need to work hard if you want to gain and retain your followers. If you want to see results and gain credibility, then you need to put in the necessary time and effort to not just create content but promote it as well. Before you create any content, take a moment to ask yourself, "Will this content be useful and if yes, then who will amplify it?" If you don't have an answer to this question or if you don't have a specific list of people, then don't create such content.

Post the Same Content on Multiple Platforms

In a bid to save time, a lot of social media users tend to create posts that they use for various social media platforms. You need to understand that no two social media platforms are alike, and you cannot post the same content everywhere. Each platform requires you to focus on different things. You can create similar content, but it is a good idea to avoid using the same content. It might be quite a challenge to create unique posts for different social media channels, especially with a constraint of time and resources, but it will be worth your while. Also, you need to understand that the audience that you have on one platform might follow you on other platforms as well. Imagine if you open Facebook, Instagram, Snapchat, and Twitter and find the same content everywhere. Your reaction might not be pleasant, and you might decide to unfollow such an account on at least one of the platforms. Well, remember that your audience will feel the same. You can use similar content but modify it according to the platform that you plan on using. For instance, can you repurpose your blog post into a YouTube video or an Instagram video? Or perhaps you can turn the data you tweeted into an infographic that you can post on Facebook.

POST AT ANY TIME OF THE DAY

It is a common myth that you can post at any given time of the day on social media. If that's what you think, then you need to think again. Certain timings are optimum when compared to the rest. There are different practices that are considered to be optimal for various social networking sites. You need to post at certain times to make sure that you receive more traffic, engagement, and followers. For instance, to increase engagement on Instagram, the ideal days to post are Thursday and Friday.

POST AS MANY TIMES AS YOU WANT ON SOCIAL MEDIA

The number of times that you can post on social media depends on the platforms that you use. You need to post at certain times to increase your visibility and engagement, and a similar rule applies to the number of times that you can post as well. You must not spam your follower's feed with numerous posts in a day. To increase your engagement, you need to post once a day or maybe twice at most. If you post frequently on any given day, your engagement rates will drop. In fact, it is a popular myth that if you schedule your posts on social media, it will result in a lower reach. On the contrary, it is important that you schedule your updates so that you can reach more people. The Internet is a global community and if you want to spread your content and increase your reach, then you need to be able to hit multiple time zones with your post. The primary objective of any post is to increase your reach. There are different social media tools that you can use to schedule a post like Buffer or Hootsuite. However, it doesn't mean that you use this as a substitute for logging in and posting in real time. Remember that it is social media and it is called so for a reason. You need to engage your followers and engagement is a two-way conversation. If you want to succeed, then you need to increase your engagement rate.

SHARE PHOTOS THAT YOU FIND ONLINE

Merely because you find something on the Internet doesn't mean that such content is public domain. You need to understand that, even when you find something online, the rights to such content or image lie with its creator. The creator owns the copyright. Keep a simple rule in mind whenever you decide to share some photo that you find online; it is covered by copyright. If you want to use something, make sure that you find the source and determine whether you can use it or not. You need to contact the creator and confirm whether you have their permission to use such an image or not. If you don't, then it is quite likely that you can run into some legal trouble regarding the infringement of copyright.

Use Corporate Voice If You Post as a Brand

It is important to maintain some professional boundaries but that doesn't mean that you don't show the human side of the brand. It is social media and, even if you post as a brand, you must not forget to highlight the personality of the brand. If you don't do this, it will reduce your engagement rate. You need to think of ways in which you can connect with your audience. A brand with a human side will appeal to an audience more than a corporate voice. Your audience needs to know that they are engaging with a human and not just a humanoid on the Internet.

Success Depends Solely on the Number of Followers

One of the parameters that you can use to gauge your success is the number of followers you have. However, it isn't the only parameter that measures your success. In fact, the quality of engagement that you have matters more than the number of followers. People tend to rashly judge their presence on social media solely based on the number of followers they have. The engagement you have with

262

your followers matters more. If you want to increase your social media presence, then there are certain things that you need to consider. For instance, how well do you know your audience? What are the topics that will appeal to your audience? How can you become the go-to resource in your niche? Whenever you create content, make sure that the audience will find it relevant and useful. The quality of content will help you attract more followers.

YOU CAN USE SOCIAL MEDIA TO REPLACE YOUR WEBSITE

You can use social media to increase your traffic and generate better leads, but it isn't the only tool that you can use. You must not ignore social media, but don't make it your only strategy to generate traffic and leads. Your bottom line must be to build your business on a given platform. You don't need a fancy website, but you need a website. Period. You can have a simple and easy-to-use website or blog that can act as a landing page. You need to encourage your visitors or followers and direct them to your website or blog.

Social media is not a stand-alone tool and you must not use it like one. Social media works well when you use it along with other marketing strategies like content marketing, SEO, and such. You need to create an integrated strategy that uses different assets, which will increase your online presence.

A lot of people believe that they cannot measure their ROI on social media. There are different tools like Google Analytics that help you identify your rate of conversion and the organic search traffic you have. You can use these metrics to not just calculate your ROI, but also to gauge the effectiveness of your marketing strategy.

Resources

Websites & Apps for the Best Instagram Tools

Below is a simple list of resources that could be used to improve the use of Instagram.

- Hyprerlase
- Develop GIFs for your Instagram Account with Boomerang
- Hootsuite Enhance
- Have2Havelt
- Hootsuite App
- Microsoft Selgie
- Pic Stitch
- Clips
- Hootsuite
- Sprout Social
- Auto Grammer
- CrowdFire

- Simply Measured

- Superimpose App

- Websta

- Vintagio

- Seekmetrics

- PLANN

- Buffer

- Font Candy

- VSCO

- Enlight

- Snapseed

- Over

- Youtube Capture

- iMovie

- Hoppe

- Facetune

- SocialDrift

- Grum

- Owlmetrics

- SnapFinch

- Bajanbot
- Woobox
- Linktree

Conclusion

Social media marketing is the way to go in this era. Whether you like it or not, a modern marketing strategy should include some aspect of social media marketing. This is because most people are nowadays using social media platforms to obtain information about the best products and services out there.

Moreover, you can long a long way to acquiring new customers from potential social media users. Instagram marketing is one of the most rampantly growing marketing aspects. It is easy to use and more and more people are getting submerged in the trend of using photos and videos for communication.

This reason has seen Instagram gain more than 1 million users in the past eight years. More people will definitely join as days go by.

Through Instagram marketing alone, you can be able to reach a minimum of about 5 million people in a single day. Even though not all will become your customers, you will develop some good will. Your business name will be known near and far. It is time to switch from traditional ways of marketing. Get digital and join the modern platforms of marketing. Try Instagram marketing and you will see the results!